The Position of the Turkish and Moroccan Second Generation

in Amsterdam and Rotterdam

IMISCOE (International Migration, Integration and Social Cohesion)

IMISCOE is a Network of Excellence uniting over 500 researchers from various institutes that specialise in migration studies across Europe. Networks of Excellence are cooperative research ventures that were created by the European Commission to help overcome the fragmentation of international studies. They amass a crucial source of knowledge and expertise to help inform European leadership today.

Since its foundation in 2004, IMISCOE has advanced an integrated, multidisciplinary and globally comparative research programme to address the themes specified in its name, short for: International Migration, Integration and Social Cohesion in Europe. IMISCOE members come from all branches of the economic and social sciences, the humanities and law. The Network draws from existing studies and advances innovative lines of inquiry key to European policy-making and governance. Priority is placed on developing a theoretical design to promote new research and offer practical alternatives for sound policy.

The IMISCOE-Amsterdam University Press Series was created to make the Network's findings and results available to researchers, policymakers, the media and the public at large. High-quality manuscripts authored by IMISCOE members and cooperating partners are published in one of four distinct series.

Research
Reports
Dissertations
Textbooks

The RESEARCH series presents empirical and theoretical scholarship addressing issues of international migration, integration and social cohesion in Europe. Authored by experts in the field, the works provide a rich reference source for researchers and other concerned parties.

The REPORTS series responds to needs for knowledge within IMISCOE's mandated fields of migration research. Compiled by leading specialists, the works disseminate succinct and timely information for European policymakers, practitioners and other stakeholders.

The DISSERTATIONS series showcases select PhD monographs written by IMISCOE doctoral candidates. The works span an array of fields within studies of international migration, integration and social cohesion in Europe.

The TEXTBOOKS series produces manuals, handbooks and other didactic tools developed by specialists in migration studies. The works are used within the IMISCOE training programme and for educational purposes by academic institutes worldwide.

IMISCOE Policy Briefs and more information on the Network can be found at www.imiscoe.org.

The Position of the Turkish and Moroccan Second Generation in Amsterdam and Rotterdam

The TIES study in the Netherlands

edited by Maurice Crul and Liesbeth Heering

IMISCOE Research

AMSTERDAM UNIVERSITY PRESS

TIES: The Integration of the European Second Generation

TIES is a collaborative and comparative research project on the descendants of immigrants from Turkey, the former Yugoslavia and Morocco who live across eight European countries: Austria, Belgium, France, Germany, the Netherlands, Spain, Sweden and Switzerland. This book is the first research report based on the TIES survey in the Netherlands, which was conducted from June 2006 through July 2007. Reports on the other participating countries will follow over the coming period.

The TIES International Overview and various PhD dissertations of students working on the TIES project are also planned for publication in the IMISCOE-AUP Series.

Cover design: Studio Jan de Boer bno, Amsterdam
Layout: The DocWorkers, Almere

ISBN   978 90 8964 061 1
e-ISBN   978 90 4850 648 4
NUR   741 / 763

© Maurice Crul and Liesbeth Heering / Amsterdam University Press, Amsterdam 2008

All rights reserved. Without limiting the rights under copyright reserved above, no part of this book may be reproduced, stored in or introduced into a retrieval system, or transmitted, in any form or by any means (electronic, mechanical, photocopying, recording or otherwise) without the written permission of both the copyright owner and the authors of the book.

Table of contents

Preface 9

Acknowledgements 11

List of tables 13

1 Introduction 19
   Maurice Crul and Liesbeth Heering
   1.1 The TIES project 19
   1.2 Theoretical and methodological backgrounds 21
   1.3 The TIES project in the Netherlands 23

2 Migration history and demographic characteristics of the two second-generation groups 27
   Gijs Beets, Susan ter Bekke and Jeannette Schoorl
   2.1 Introduction 27
   2.2 Immigration trends and migration policy: a brief historic overview 27
   2.3 People of Turkish and Moroccan descent in Amsterdam and Rotterdam 31
   2.4 Demographic characteristics of the second generation in the TIES survey 34
      2.4.1 Demographic characteristics of the second generation 34
      2.4.2 Demographic characteristics of the parents 36
      2.4.3 Demographic characteristics of the siblings 42
      2.4.4 Household size and position 43
   2.5 Conclusions 45

3 Housing and segregation 49
   Carlo van Praag and Jeannette Schoorl
   3.1 Introduction 49
   3.2 Housing situation 49
   3.3 Concentration and segregation 52
   3.4 Housing policies 54
   3.5 Housing situation of the second generation 56
   3.6 Conclusions 62

4	Education	63
	Helga de Valk and Maurice Crul	
	4.1 Introduction	63
	4.2 The educational system in the Netherlands	63
	4.3 Educational priority policies in the Netherlands	65
	4.4 Overview of the educational position of pupils and students of Moroccan and Turkish descent	66
	4.5 TIES respondents: entry into school	67
	4.6 Primary education	68
	4.7 Secondary education	72
	4.8 Experiences at school	77
	4.9 The parental home and education	80
	4.10 Conclusions	84
5	Labour and income	87
	Liesbeth Heering and Susan ter Bekke	
	5.1 Introduction	87
	5.2 Ethnic minorities in labour market policies	87
	5.3 The labour market position of Turks and Moroccans in Amsterdam and Rotterdam	90
	5.4 Labour market position of the three study groups in the TIES survey	91
	5.5 Income position of the three ethnic groups in the TIES survey	97
	5.6 Discrimination on the labour market	99
	5.7 Conclusions	102
6	Identities and intercultural relations	105
	George Groenewold	
	6.1 Introduction	105
	6.2 Dutch context of identity and intercultural relations	106
	6.3 Indicators of identity	108
	6.4 Language proficiency and use	112
	6.5 Religion	113
	6.5.1 Affiliation with religion	113
	6.5.2 Religiosity	114
	6.6 Transnationalism	119
	6.7 Intercultural relations	120
	6.7.1 Preferred norms and values	120
	6.7.2 Views on the multicultural society	121
	6.7.3 Views on members of other ethnic and social groups	123
	6.8 Conclusions	124

7	Social relations *Liesbeth Heering and Susan ter Bekke*		129
	7.1	Introduction	129
	7.2	Ethnic character of friendships in secondary school and at present	129
	7.3	Participation in and ethnic orientation of social organisations	132
	7.4	Perceptions on personal and group discrimination	134
	7.5	Conclusions	140
8	Union and family formation *Helga de Valk*		143
	8.1	Introduction	143
	8.2	The context of union and family formation among immigrants	143
	8.3	Union formation among the TIES respondents: timing and type of current relationships	145
	8.4	Meeting places and family influence	148
	8.5	Partner choice: partner characteristics	149
	8.6	Family formation	153
	8.7	Task division	154
	8.8	Conclusions	158
9	Conclusions and implications *Maurice Crul, George Groenewold and Liesbeth Heering*		161
	9.1	Study implications	165
Appendix:	Sample design, TIES survey implementation and evaluation *George Groenewold*		169
	1.1	Sample design	169
	1.2	TIES survey implementation	175
	1.3	TIES survey evaluation	176
Conclusies en aanbevelingen *Maurice Crul, George Groenewold en Liesbeth Heering*			181
List of contributors			189

Preface

This is the first publication of The Integration of the European Second generation international project known as TIES. The project started in 2003 with a preliminary study, funded by the Swiss Stiftung für Bevölkerung, Migration und Umwelt (BMU), which allowed us to form the TIES study group, comprising partners from eight European countries. Maurice Crul and Hans Vermeulen from the Institute for Migration and Ethnic Studies (IMES) at the University of Amsterdam acted as the first international coordinators of the TIES team. Jens Schneider succeeded Hans Vermeulen upon his retirement. The Netherlands Interdisciplinary Demographic Institute (NIDI) was made responsible for the international coordination of the TIES survey. Jeannette Schoorl and Ernst Spaan were the first NIDI tandem for this particular task, with Liesbeth Heering and George Groenewold eventually taking over. During 2004 and 2005, the TIES study group met in four international workshops to discuss the development of a common research design.

The next step was to secure funding for the TIES survey itself. The German Volkswagen Stiftung was the first to support our efforts by granting funds for a core part of the project: a survey held in five countries among second-generation Turks and a native comparison group. Additional national and international funding requests (including two ESF ECRP applications) enabled the TIES group to add three more countries and to include two additional groups. The budget for the coordination and implementation of the survey now totals about 2.5 million euros. Funding agencies in the Netherlands include NWO and NWO-ESF EUROCORES, the Ministry of Justice (DCIM), the cities of Amsterdam and Rotterdam as well as the Royal Academy of Sciences of the Netherlands. Their funding enabled us to start the TIES project in 2005.

From the very start, a principal objective of the TIES team has been to produce policy-relevant outcomes and to communicate these outcomes to policymakers, migrant organisations and other relevant actors on the local, national and European levels. Publication of a second TIES report is expected to coincide with this Dutch country report. The former will be launched by the National Urban Knowledge Centre (KIEM) under the title of *De Tweede Generatie: Last of Kapitaal voor de Steden*

('*The Second Generation: A Burden or a Source of Capital for the Cities*'). A draft version of this manuscript, which addresses the issues at stake for 'at-risk' and successful second-generation youth, provided the input for a workshop in May 2008 with policymakers and representatives of immigrant organisations from Amsterdam and Rotterdam. The Dutch country report and the ultimate KIEM publication will be used as input for the national round table conference on the TIES project in October 2008.

The Dutch country report is only one in a series of eight such reports that are due to be published in 2008 and 2009. The international dimension is, of course, the most important added value of the TIES project. For the first time ever, we will be able to compare the Dutch second generation with other second generations in as many as seven other European countries. A number of international comparative publications are expected to follow – among which are as many as fifteen PhD theses.

Acknowledgements

We would like to express our gratitude to our sponsors and institutes for their invaluable support to the TIES project. We would like to thank a few people in particular. Alinda Bosch was a crucial sparring partner; she provided indispensable help at the time the questionnaire and instructions for the interviewers had to be put in their final format. Frans Lelie has been involved from the project's very beginning, and we thank her for translating the questionnaire and the concluding chapter into Dutch. Yolanda Schothorst and her staff from Bureau Veldkamp, the interviewers and the respondents of the TIES survey in Amsterdam and in Rotterdam devoted a lot of time and energy to provide us with valuable information and insights. We are extremely grateful for the very rich source of material they made available to us. Jens Schneider was an important source of advice and help for the book's identity chapter as well as its final chapter. Laetis Kuipers critically scrutinised the English language in parts of the manuscript, and Jaqueline van der Helm tirelessly formatted our texts and tables into the proper layout. We would also like to thank Karina Hof for performing a final copyedit on the manuscript.

Maurice Crul, International Coordinator of the TIES project
Liesbeth Heering, International Coordinator of the TIES survey

List of tables

Table 1.1	Sample sizes aimed at in different countries and cities, by ethnic group	23
Table 2.1	Age distribution, by ethnic group and sex in Amsterdam	35
Table 2.2	Age distribution, by ethnic group and sex in Rotterdam	35
Table 2.3	Citizenship, by ethnic group	36
Table 2.4	Neighbourhood of residence during early to mid-teens (ages 12-16), by ethnic group	36
Table 2.5	Parents' country of birth, by ethnic group	37
Table 2.6	Parents' year of immigration, by ethnic group	38
Table 2.7	Parents' duration of residence in the Netherlands, by ethnic group	39
Table 2.8	Parents' citizenship, by ethnic group	40
Table 2.9	Parents' (highest) level of education, by ethnic group	41
Table 2.10	Mother/father worked before migrating to the Netherlands, by ethnic group	41
Table 2.11	Occupation of father before migration to the Netherlands, according to SBC classification, by ethnic group	42
Table 2.12	Number of siblings, by ethnic group	42
Table 2.13	Household size, by ethnic group and type of household	43
Table 2.14	Household composition, by ethnic group and sex	44
Table 2.15	Reasons for leaving the parental home in %, by ethnic group	44
Table 3.1	Some characteristics of the housing stock, 2004	50
Table 3.2	Dwelling characteristics of ethnic groups in Amsterdam, Rotterdam and the Netherlands	51
Table 3.3	Ownership and rent levels of the Turkish/Moroccan and Dutch populations (in multiple-person households)	51
Table 3.4	Segregation of Turks and Moroccans in Amsterdam and Rotterdam, 1 January 2007	54
Table 3.5	Household composition, by ethnic group and sex	56

Table 3.6	Home ownership and rental structure, by living arrangement and ethnic group	57
Table 3.7	Type of dwelling, by living arrangement and ethnic group	58
Table 3.8	Construction period of dwellings, by living arrangement and ethnic group	58
Table 3.9	Living arrangements and housing characteristics, by ethnic group	59
Table 3.10	Degree of neighbourhood concentration, by living arrangement and ethnic group	59
Table 3.11	Living arrangements and neighbourhood preferences, by ethnic group	60
Table 3.12	Actual and preferred prevalence level of own ethnic group members in neighbourhood, by ethnic group	60
Table 3.13	Per cent agreeing or strongly agreeing with statement on the quality of life in the neighbourhoods, by living arrangement and ethnic group	61
Table 4.1	Entry into preschool or school, by age and mean ages	68
Table 4.2	Attendance of preschool, by ethnic group and age group	68
Table 4.3	Reasons given for choosing a primary school in %, by ethnic group	69
Table 4.4	Share of children of immigrants at primary school, by ethnic group and age group	70
Table 4.5	Ever repeated classes, by ethnic group and sex	71
Table 4.6	Percentage ever spent more than three months abroad during primary education, by age group and ethnic group	71
Table 4.7	School advice at the end of primary education, by ethnic group	72
Table 4.8	Reasons given for choosing a secondary school in %, by ethnic group	73
Table 4.9	Share of children of immigrants at secondary school, by ethnic group and age group	74
Table 4.10	Ever changed secondary schools, by city of residence and ethnic group	74
Table 4.11	Ever repeated classes, by ethnic group	75
Table 4.12a	Highest educational level for those currently not in education, by ethnic group and sex	76
Table 4.12b	Current educational level for those who are in education, by ethnic group and sex	77
Table 4.13	Ever had remedial teaching or homework counselling at secondary school in %, by ethnic group	78

LIST OF TABLES

Table 4.14	Description of relationships with teachers, by ethnic group	79
Table 4.15	Description of others' impact on education while in secondary school, by ethnic group and sex	81
Table 4.16	Involvement of parents in schooling, by ethnic group and sex	83
Table 5.1	Working-age population with paid work in Amsterdam and Rotterdam in %, by age group, ethnic group and generation, 2004	90
Table 5.2	Working-age population with social benefits in Amsterdam and Rotterdam in %, by age group, ethnic group and generation, 2004	91
Table 5.3	Labour situation, by ethnic group and sex	92
Table 5.4	Situation after finishing education and before first job, by ethnic group and sex	93
Table 5.5	SBC level of current job for those who finished education, by ethnic group	94
Table 5.6a	Average prestige score (U&S-92) of current jobs for those who have finished education, by ethnic group and sex	94
Table 5.6b	Average prestige score (U&S-92) of current jobs for those who have finished education, by ethnic group and age group	94
Table 5.7	Future plans concerning working career of those who do paid work, by ethnic group and sex	96
Table 5.8	Reception of benefits, by ethnic group	97
Table 5.9	Net monthly income from employment for those who finished education, by ethnic group and sex	98
Table 5.10	Net monthly income from employment, by living arrangement and ethnic group	98
Table 5.11	Perceived personal discrimination in finding a job, by ethnic group and sex	100
Table 5.12	Perceived personal discrimination at the workplace, by ethnic group and sex	101
Table 5.13	Perceived group discrimination of Turks and Moroccans in finding a job, by ethnic group and city	101
Table 6.1	Identification of respondents with different types of social and spatial entities, by ethnic group and sex	109
Table 6.2	Description of feelings of belonging to Islam combined with feelings of belonging to the Netherlands and to Amsterdam or Rotterdam, by ethnic group	111

Table 6.3	Self-reported proficiency in Dutch language and ethnic group language, by ethnic group	112
Table 6.4	Religious affiliation, by ethnic group	114
Table 6.5	Secularisation trends and differentials: religious affiliation during upbringing and current status, by ethnic group	114
Table 6.6	Perceptions on importance of religion in personal life, by ethnic group	116
Table 6.7	Perceptions on role of religion in wider society and importance given to the use of religious symbols outside the home, by ethnic group	117
Table 6.8	Perceptions regarding whether people of immigrant origin have the right to live as much as possible in accordance with the cultural customs and norms of their country of origin or the Netherlands, by ethnic group	120
Table 6.9	Perceptions on the multicultural society, by ethnic group	122
Table 6.10	Rating of feelings towards other social groups on a thermometer scale (0-100°), by ethnic group	123
Table 7.1	Ethnic diversity in best friends at secondary school, by ethnic group	130
Table 7.2	Number of Dutch friends at secondary school among second-generation Turks and Moroccans and number of Turkish and Moroccan friends at secondary school among comparison group members	131
Table 7.3	Ethnic diversity in current best friends, by ethnic group	131
Table 7.4	Number of current Dutch friends among second-generation Turks and Moroccans and number of current Turkish and Moroccan friends among comparison group members	132
Table 7.5	Number of organisations (maximum of 9) in which activities were undertaken over the past year, by ethnic group and city	133
Table 7.6	Top three organisations in which activities were undertaken by second-generation Turks and Moroccans and whether or not they are oriented towards their own ethnic group	134
Table 7.7	Personal experience with discrimination, by ethnic group	135
Table 7.8	Top three situations of experiencing personal discrimination, by ethnic group and sex	136

LIST OF TABLES

Table 7.9	Top three groups in society that are perceived to be discriminated against, by ethnic group and city	138
Table 7.10	Top three situations in which Turks and Moroccans are perceived to be discriminated against, by ethnic group	139
Table 8.1	Young adults living with or without a partner in the same household, by ethnic group and sex	146
Table 8.2	Mean age and age difference between partners when starting to live with current partner, by ethnic group and sex	146
Table 8.3	Mean age at marriage to current partner, by ethnic group and sex	147
Table 8.4	Place of meeting current partner, by ethnic group	148
Table 8.5	Family influences on decision-making regarding marriage, by ethnic group	149
Table 8.6	Origin of partner, by ethnic group and age group	150
Table 8.7	Couples with same educational level, by ethnic group	151
Table 8.8	Family links between partners, by ethnic group	152
Table 8.9	Current situation of the partner, by ethnic group and sex of the respondent	152
Table 8.10	Current number of children and mean age at birth of first child, by ethnic group	154
Table 8.11	Division of tasks in the household, by ethnic group	155
Table 8.12	Whether respondents are happy with division of tasks between household partners, by ethnic group and sex	156
Table 8.13	Labour force participation of men and women before birth of first child, by ethnic group	157
Table 8.14	Change in labour force participation after childbirth, by ethnic group and sex	157
Table A.1	Reference population, sample design and implementation statistics of study groups in Amsterdam and Rotterdam	174
Table A.2	Differences between respondents and non-respondents regarding characteristics recorded in municipal population registers (GBA)	177

1 Introduction

Maurice Crul and Liesbeth Heering

Immigration, combined with the subsequent integration of newcomers, forms one of the foremost challenges to Europe's increasingly heterogeneous cities. Second-generation integration – meaning integration by children of immigrant parentage born in the country of migration – is crucial to this process, for it is these children who constitute a growing share of metropolitan youth today. Thus, research on second-generation issues is particularly pertinent because it may answer many current-day integration questions. In theory, second-generation children should have the same chances and opportunities as children of native-born parents. In determining whether or not this is the case, the relative position of second-generation members with regard to education and labour force participation is often viewed as a robust measure of group integration as a whole. The older children born to labour migrants are now finishing their educational careers and are beginning to enter the labour market in considerable numbers. The first true assessment of second-generation integration can now be made.

This publication on the Dutch situation investigates how the integration of second generations is proceeding in various domains, including housing, education, the labour market, social relations and finally identity and family formation. Section 1.1 gives an introduction to the history of TIES project. Section 1.2 describes the project's theoretical and methodological backgrounds, and Section 1.3 provides details about the Dutch study.

1.1 The TIES project

The year 2005 saw the birth of a comprehensive international research project on second generations in eight European countries. It was named 'TIES', an acronym for The Integration of the European Second generation (www.tiesproject.eu). The general project coordination was put in the hands of the Institute for Migration and Ethnic Studies (IMES) at the University of Amsterdam. The Netherlands Interdisciplinary Demographic Institute (NIDI) was given the task of coordinating the international survey included in the TIES project.

TIES studies the descendants of immigrants from Turkey, the former Yugoslavia and Morocco in seven EU member states and Switzerland. The term 'second generation' here refers to those children of immigrants who were born in the country of immigration and who are currently aged between eighteen and 35. For the purpose of comparison, a group of native-born age peers has been included, of whom *both* parents were born in the survey country itself. In our publications, the latter group is referred to as 'the comparison group'. This label, as opposed to other options like 'native Dutch' or simply 'Dutch', was chosen for two reasons: firstly, the second-generation Turks, Moroccans and former Yugoslavs also included in the study are, by definition, native-born and many, if not the majority, have the nationality of the country of birth. Secondly, some members of our comparison group are themselves of mixed ethnic background. In the Netherlands, for instance, the group also includes respondents of 'third-generation' Surinamese or Indonesian background, to name but two examples.

The criterion of ethnic group used in the TIES study and throughout this report is therefore a purely demographic one. In this report, the terms 'Turkish' and 'Moroccan' simply refer to the fact that either one or both of the respondents' parents were born in Turkey or Morocco: the terms do *not* index ethnic and/or national belonging or citizenship, and are explicitly not a juxtaposition to 'being Dutch'. Likewise, being a member of the comparison group only refers to the fact that *both* parents were born in the Netherlands: such membership should not be understood as a synonym for 'Dutch' or 'native'.

We are aware of the fact that many immigrants from Morocco or Turkey identify themselves with categories other than national ones. Within the Turkish second-generation group of our study, there is a small group of respondents identifying itself as Kurdish, and in the Moroccan second generation, there is considerable group identifying itself as Berber. We found, however, that in both second-generation groups, identification with these minority categories blend well with self-identification as Turkish or Moroccan (see the chapter on identities for more specific results in this regard).

Since migration presents itself primarily as an urban phenomenon, the TIES project is currently being realised in fifteen cities across eight countries: Paris and Strasbourg in France; Berlin and Frankfurt in Germany; Madrid and Barcelona in Spain; Vienna and Linz in Austria; Amsterdam and Rotterdam in the Netherlands; Brussels and Antwerp in Belgium; Zurich and Basle in Switzerland; Stockholm in Sweden. In the majority of the cities, the focus will fall on three different groups: two second-generation groups and a comparison group. The two respective second-generation groups consist of people of Turkish or Moroccan descent living in the Netherlands and Belgium and people of Turkish or former Yugoslavian descent living in Germany, Austria and Switzerland. In France and Sweden, funding could only be secured for one second-generation group (consisting of people of Turkish descent) and a comparison group. Due to the fact that the influx of labour migrants in Spain occurred at a later stage, the Spanish project will only include Moroccans and a comparison group.

Most of the comparative European studies on integration carried out so far have focused on immigrants in general. The heterogeneity associated with the categories 'immigrants' or 'children of immigrants' makes it difficult to ensure truly international comparability. Studying specific ethnic groups with similar starting positions (in this case, being part of the second generation) makes it easier to draw up cross-national comparisons and to assess the importance of the *receiving context* in integration processes. The TIES project aims to analyse the relative effects of specific city and national contexts in promoting or hampering the integration of the second generation.

1.2 Theoretical and methodological backgrounds

The study of the second generation in Europe will test key assumptions on integration and integration theory. Stemming from different theoretical perspectives, our analytical grid seeks to test a range of hypotheses and will address major theoretical issues in the debates on integration. We believe this will be the most effective strategy for our research.

We make use of two theoretical approaches in particular: the citizenship approach and the institutional approach. The citizenship approach assumes that national immigration and integration policies constitute one of the major determinants of the integration process (Brubaker 1992; Castles & Miller 1993; Joppke 1999). This approach is of particular relevance for issues such as ethnic and religious identity formation, transnationalism and family formation and partner choice (Heckmann et al. 2001). At the same time, the institutional approach seems particularly suited for the study of structural integration. A number of the senior researchers in our project team (Crul & Vermeulen 2003, 2006; Crul & Doomernik 2003; Herzog-Punzenserger 2003; Simon 2003) developed this new line of thinking in a special issue of *International Migration Review* (no. 37, vol. 4) (Crul & Vermeulen 2003, 2006). These authors show that variations in educational and labour market status can be linked to differences in national educational institutional arrangements (starting age of compulsory schooling, number of school contact hours in primary school, school system characteristics and practices of early or late selection in secondary education) and different ways of formalising transitions to the labour market (in particular, the emphasis placed on apprenticeship systems) in the respective countries (cf. Faist 1995; Muus 2003).

The second-generation groups in the TIES project not only belong to an ethnic minority group, but also find themselves in a very low class position. This has prompted a discussion on the role of class and culture in integration problems and whether or not these two factors are intertwined in ways that are difficult to unpack analytically (Crul & Thomson 2007).

A further question is how cultural and structural integration interrelate. Do cultural maintenance and a strong ethnic identity hamper socioeconomic integration, or do they generate cultural and social capital that facilitates it? We will try to determine how relevant the theory of segmented assimilation (Portes & Rumbaut 2001) is to the European context.[1]

Gender will occupy a prominent place in our study. As we tentatively established in *International Migration Review*'s special issue on the second generation in Europe, the educational careers of second-generation adolescents differ according to gender in the three ethnic target groups, and labour market careers of male and female young adults differ from country to country.

The central aim of the TIES project is to provide what would be the first systematic cross-national comparison of the second generation in Europe. This kind of internationally comparative, empirically grounded research into integration processes is still very rare, especially because it is technically very complicated, and almost no infrastructure exists for such work. As a first step in the TIES project, a common questionnaire for administration in all eight countries was developed. Its main topics include education, labour market position, income, housing, ethnic and religious identity, social relations, gender roles, partner choice and transnationalism. In all modules, questions on experiences related to discrimination take up a prominent position. In addition to the international survey, the national partners gathered information on national and local institutional arrangements as well as general and group-specific policies (including anti-discrimination schemes) targeting the children of immigrants.

In each country, we held interviews with 500 members of each ethnic group, divided across the participating cities, and 500 members of the same age included in the comparison groups. Table 1.1 gives an overview of the targets set for the survey in the eight countries involved.

INTRODUCTION

Table 1.1 *Sample sizes aimed at in different countries and cities, by ethnic group*

	Turkish second generation	Moroccan second generation	Former Yugoslavian second generation	Comparison group	Total
Sweden					500
Stockholm	250	0	0	250	
Germany					1,500
Berlin	250	0	250	250	
Frankfurt	250	0	250	250	
The Netherlands					1,500
Amsterdam	250	250	0	250	
Rotterdam	250	250	0	250	
Belgium					1,500
Antwerp	250	250	0	250	
Brussels	250	250	0	250	
France					1,000
Paris	250	0	0	250	
Strasbourg	250	0	0	250	
Spain					1,000
Madrid	0	250	0	250	
Barcelona	0	250	0	250	
Austria					1,500
Vienna	250	0	250	250	
Linz	250	0	250	250	
Switzerland					1,500
Basle	250	0	250	250	
Zurich	250	0	250	250	
Total	3,250	1,500	1,500	3,750	10,000

1.3 The TIES project in the Netherlands

The Netherlands, especially when compared with other European countries, has so far conducted an impressive amount of research on the position of immigrants and their children. Until recently, the most important survey in the Netherlands was the 'Sociale Positie en Voorzieningengebruik Allochtonen' (SPVA), which was meant to assess the social position and use of public services by immigrants. This survey was repeated every four years from 1988 to 2002. It focused on the four major immigrant groups (Surinamese, Antilleans, Moroccans and Turks) residing in the Netherlands. SPVA findings have frequently been used for the periodic compilation of national minority reports, the main source of information on immigrants and their children in the Netherlands. In the SPVA, household heads were interviewed by means of an extensive questionnaire; their partners and children were given a shorter questionnaire. The survey focused on four major cities and nine medium-sized cities.

The 'Survey Integratie Minderheden' (SIM) on minority integration recently replaced the SPVA survey (Dagevos et al. 2007). While the SPVA targeted heads of households for most of the information collected, SIM made use of a national sample of individuals. This constitutes a fundamental change, resulting in a more equal gender distribution in SIM compared with the earlier SPVA surveys. However, since SIM is a national survey, it also means that fewer cases are covered in the larger cities.

The TIES survey targets individuals in a particular age range, rather than heads of households. It was designed in such a way that members of the three ethnic groups (i.e. second-generation Turks, Moroccans and the comparison group) were sampled in the same context: that is, in the same neighbourhood in each city. The number of second-generation interviewees from Amsterdam and Rotterdam included in the TIES survey equals the number of both in-between and second-generation youth aged fifteen and over in the SIM survey for the whole of the Netherlands. The fact that SIM intends to include people above the age of 35 means that SIM's in-between generation will be substantive. The ultimate actual overlap in eighteen- to 35-year-old respondents of the second generation will therefore be small. Obviously, the SIM survey of 2006 is the best national reference point with which to compare the TIES survey findings. Both surveys were conducted by Bureau Veldkamp in Amsterdam. Procedures followed in the field were therefore highly similar. A complete technical description of the sampling procedures and the fieldwork of the TIES survey can be found in Appendix 1. In close cooperation with IMES, NIDI was responsible for the fieldwork carried out in the Netherlands.

Compared with the SIM survey, the most important added value of the TIES survey is its exclusive focus on second-generation youth. The larger number of second-generation youth included in the TIES survey allows more complex analyses for this group in particular. Also new in the Dutch context is the detailed gathering of timeline data related to education and the labour market, which makes it possible to reconstruct school and labour market careers. Another important difference of the TIES survey is its focus on the two largest cities in the Netherlands. This makes our findings especially interesting for Amsterdam and Rotterdam.

This particular TIES publication for the Netherlands contains first, basic and mainly descriptive findings on all the main topics of the Dutch TIES survey. Most chapters start with a short description of the relevant structural and policy contexts of the issues at hand. The background information on, for instance, labour market policies or the Dutch educational system has a twofold purpose: it serves not only as a basis for interpreting survey results, but also as an introduction to some of the basic features of the Dutch (policy) context for a non-Dutch audience. This volume ends with a concluding chapter in which our main findings are discussed and related to one another. A Dutch translation of this particular chapter (especially for the benefit of our Dutch readership) can be found at the back of this volume.

More complex analyses of specific topics will be published in TIES papers and articles, comparative publications and PhD studies. Most of these follow-up publications will be made available through the TIES website: www.tiesproject.eu.

Note

1   For the debate on segmented assimilation, see Alba and Nee (2003); Crul and Vermeulen (2003); Waldinger and Perlmann (1998); Vermeulen and Perlmann (2000).

References

Alba, R. & V. Nee (2003), *Remaking the American Mainstream: Assimilation and Contemporary Immigration*. Cambridge: Harvard University Press.

Brubaker, W.R. (1992), *Citizenship and Nationhood in France and Germany*. Cambridge: Harvard University Press.

Castles, S. & M.J. Miller (1993), *The Age of Migration. International Population Movements in the Modern World*. London: Macmillan.

Crul, M. & J. Doomernik (2003), 'The Turkish and the Moroccan second generation in the Netherlands: Divergent trends between and polarization within the two groups', *International Migration Review* 37(4): 1039-1065.

Crul, M. & M. Thomson (2007), The Second Generation in Europe and the United States: How is the Transatlantic Debate Relevant for Further Research on the European Second Generation?, *Journal of Ethnic and Migration Studies* 33(7): 1025-1041.

Crul, M. & H. Vermeulen (2003), 'The Second Generation in Europe. Introduction', *International Migration Review* 37(4): 965-986.

Crul, M. & H. Vermeulen (2006), 'Immigration, education, and the Turkish second generation in five European nations. A comparative study', in C.A Parsons & T.M. Smeeding (eds.), *Immigration and the Transformation of Europe*, 236-250. Cambridge: Cambridge University Press.

Dagevos, J.M., M. Gijsberts, J. Kappelhof & M. Vervoort (2007), *Survey Integratie Minderheden. Verantwoording van de opzet en de uitvoering van een survey onder Turken, Marokkanen, Surinmaers, Antillianen en een autochtone vergelijkingsgroep*. The Hague: Sociaal en Cultureel Planbureau.

Faist, T. (1995), *Social Citizenship for Whom? Young Turks in Germany and Mexican-Americans in the United States*. Aldershot: Avebury.

Heckmann, F., H.W. Lederer & S. Worbs (2001), *Effectiveness of National Integration Strategies towards Second Generation Migrant Youth in a Comparative European Perspective. Final Report to the European Commission*. Bamberg: EFMS.

Herzog-Punzensberger, B. (2003), 'Ethnic Segmentation in School and Labour Market – 40 year Legacy of Austrian "Guestworker" Policy', *International Migration Review* 37 (4): 1120-1144.

Joppke, C. (1999), *Immigration and the Nation-State: The United States, Germany and Great Britain*. Oxford: Oxford University Press.

Muus, P. (2003), *Migration- and Immigrant Policy, Immigrants from Turkey and Their Participation in the Labour Market: An International Comparison*. Utrecht: ERCOMER.

Portes, A. & R. Rumbaut (2001), *Legacies: The Story of the Immigrant Second Generation*. Berkeley: University of California Press.

Simon, P. (2003), 'France and the Unknown Second Generation: Preliminary results on Social Mobility', *International Migration Review* 37(4): 1091-1119.

Vermeulen, H. & P. Penninx (eds.) (2000), *Immigrant Integration: The Dutch Case*. Amsterdam: Het Spinhuis.

Vermeulen, H. & J. Perlmann (2000), *Immigrants schooling and social mobility. Does culture make a difference?* London: MacMillan.

Waldinger, R. & J. Perlmann (1998), 'Second generation: Past, present, future', *Journal of Ethnic and Migration Studies* 24(1): 5-24.

2 Migration history and demographic characteristics of the two second-generation groups

Gijs Beets, Susan ter Bekke and Jeannette Schoorl

2.1 Introduction

To improve understanding of the second generation, this chapter reviews the history and demography of the Turkish and Moroccan groups. It looks in more detail at why they happen to be as large as they are in the two major cities of the Netherlands, where their parents originate and how the two groups are composed demographically. Where possible, the two groups are contrasted with the comparison group (i.e. persons with both parents born in the Netherlands). Section 2.2 deals with immigration trends and migration policies in the Netherlands, while Section 2.3 describes the size and age-sex composition of the population of Turkish and Moroccan descent in Amsterdam and in Rotterdam. Section 2.4 provides a further breakdown of demographic characteristics among second-generation Turks and Moroccans in Amsterdam and in Rotterdam, and section 2.5 draws conclusions.

2.2 Immigration trends and migration policy: a brief historic overview[1]

Up until the 1970s, the Netherlands did not consider itself an immigration country, although, from the early 1960s onwards, more people were entering the country than leaving it. As a consequence of the economic boom following the end of World War II, labour shortages in the industrial sector led to an increasing demand for low-skilled workers. As a temporary solution, low-skilled male workers were recruited from southern European countries such as Italy (1960) and Spain (1961), and later on also from Turkey (1964) and Morocco (1969). Many of these so-called 'guest workers' worked in the textile industries, road construction and other labour-intensive sectors (Van Amersfoort 1986; Nicolaas et al. 2003) and settled in Amsterdam, Rotterdam, Utrecht and cities in Twente and Brabant (Butter 2000).

Figure 2.1 shows the immigration of people with Turkish or Moroccan citizenship from 1969 onwards. Since the presence of these guest workers was considered a temporary solution to labour shortages, both by the government and the migrants themselves, the immigrants arrived 'alone', leaving their families behind and hoping to return to their home country after a few years (Van Amersfoort 1986). The oil crisis in 1973 and the following economic downfall put an end to the recruitments from abroad. Most Spanish and Italian guest workers returned to their country of origin due to positive economic developments in their home countries, but many Turks and Moroccans stayed in the Netherlands (Van Wissen & De Beer 2000). From 1973 onwards, the immigration from Turkey and Morocco increased. In addition to some illegal labour migration, this was mainly the result of family reunification and – later on – family formation (Nicolaas et al. 2003). The share of female immigrants from Turkey and Morocco rapidly increased to over 50 per cent (see Figure 2.2), with the exception of 1975 when, as a consequence of a one-time regularisation procedure, almost 15,000 illegal workers (mostly male and about half of them Turks or Moroccans) received a legal status (Nicolaas & Spangers 2000).[2]

In 1980, immigration from Turkey and Morocco reached a peak, when 17,500 Turks and 10,400 Moroccans immigrated to the Netherlands. In the early 1980s, more restrictive labour migration policies were introduced, which channelled the entrance of high-skilled immigrants. This proved beneficial to the Dutch labour market and prohibited low-skilled migration (Bruquetas-Callejo et al. 2007). Furthermore, a visa requirement was introduced for Turks and Moroccans, and stricter rules were set for family reunification (Van Wissen & De Beer 2000). Both these measures and the economic recession were probably what resulted in a

Figure 2.1 *Immigration of persons with Turkish or Moroccan citizenship, 1969-2006*

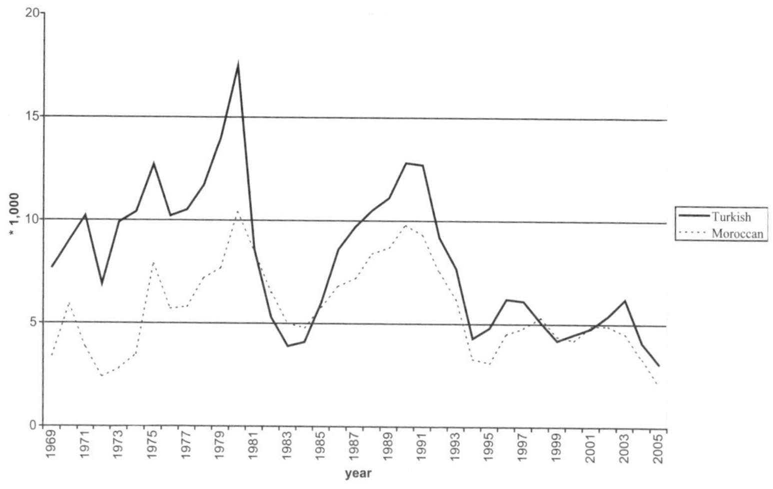

Source: Statistics Netherlands

Figure 2.2 *Share of female immigrants, by citizenship (Turkish or Moroccan), 1969-2006*

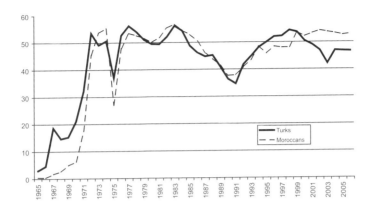

Source: Statistics Netherlands

substantial drop in immigration from Turkey and Morocco: in 1984 only 4,800 Moroccans and 4,100 Turks immigrated into the Netherlands.

Besides changes in labour migration, a new integration policy was instituted. In their report on *Ethnic Minorities* (Wetenschappelijke Raad voor het Regeringsbeleid 1979), the Scientific Council for Government Policy pleaded for recognition of the fact that several immigrant groups had settled in an effectively permanent way in the Netherlands and most likely would not return to their country of origin (Van Amersfoort 1986). This led to the ethnic minorities policy report *Minderhedennota* (Ministerie van Binnenlandse Zaken 1983), which proposed equality in the socio-economic domain (particularly in the labour market, education and housing), and paid particular attention to women and youth. Already by the end of the 1980s, these policies were being criticised mainly for their failure to integrate the ethnic minorities in the labour and education domains. It was thought that policies had been too strongly focused on subsidising migrant organisations. Family reunification and, in particular, marriage migration (family formation migration) were now perceived as a problem that hindered the integration of individuals and families in Dutch society. Nevertheless, in the second half of the 1980s immigration of Turks and Moroccans increased again, as the result of further marriage migration and continuing economic growth. Family migration increased in the second half of the 1980s. By the early 1990s, migration overall started to decrease, as did shares of women migrants.

Statistics Netherlands is one of the few statistical offices in the world to employ a definition of the immigrant and indigenous population that includes information on the native-born descendants of immigrants. The Dutch population registers collect information on country of birth and citizenship, as well as on country of birth of both parents. Statistics Netherlands refers to *'allochtonen'*, or persons of foreign descent, as those who were either born abroad themselves (the 'first generation') or those who were born in the Netherlands to at least one parent born abroad (the 'second generation'). The population of Turkish descent in 2007 now amounts to 364,300 and that of Moroccan descent to 323,200.

There is considerable discrepancy between outcomes of data by country of birth, by nationality and by descent (i.e. the combination of data by country of birth and parents' country of birth). In 2006, for instance, according to data from Statistics Netherlands, the number of Turkish citizens in the Netherlands was 86,200, and the number born in Turkey (irrespective of nationality) was more than twice as large (196,000). The population of Turkish descent was again almost twice as large: 364,300. For Moroccans, the figures are comparable: 98,900 (citizens), 168,600 (country of birth) and 323,200 (descent).

The difference between these figures is to a large extent due to the combined effect of naturalisation trends and fertility. According to Dutch law, the main way to obtain Dutch nationality is through birth to a Dutch father (*ius sanguini*) or, since 1985, to a Dutch mother. Before the Nationality Act of 2003, foreigners who applied for the naturalisation procedure were granted citizenship if they had (legally) resided in the Netherlands for at least five years, had a sufficient command of the Dutch language and were clear of serious criminal record (Groenendijk 2004). With the Nationality Act of 2003 some further restrictions were introduced, the most important of which is the formal naturalisation exam in which the applicant's degree of integration is tested. Such restrictions led to a 67 per cent decrease in applications between 2002 and 2004. About half of the applicants failed the test, while under the more lenient pre-2003 rules, only 1 to 2 per cent of the applications were denied for reasons of insufficient integration. The requirement to renounce one's original nationality was temporarily abolished (1992-1997); the 2003 act also lists a number of exemptions. Currently, 63 per cent of those acquiring citizenship through the naturalisation procedure keep their original nationality (Van Oers et al. 2006). For those with Moroccan nationality, this is up to 100 per cent, as they cannot even renounce their citizenship, according to Moroccan law.

The third generation (i.e. grandchildren of immigrants) do not have to apply for naturalisation. They receive Dutch citizenship automatically based on the principle of *ius soli*, i.e. their birth in the Netherlands. The Nationality Act of 2003 also provides for the possibility of the second generation acquiring Dutch nationality, based on the same principle. Since 1985, children of immigrants – if they were born in the Netherlands and have resided in the country since birth – may also receive Dutch citizenship by the simpler 'option' procedure. This procedure was extended to several other categories in the Nationality Act of 2003. The option procedure is less rigorous in the sense that it exempts applicants from the integration requirement and the obligation to renounce one's original nationality. However, since 2003's act came into effect, an investigation of public order is nonetheless instituted and a fee is charged, just as in the regular naturalisation procedure (Van Oers et al. 2006).

2.3 People of Turkish and Moroccan descent in Amsterdam and Rotterdam

The TIES project was carried out in the two largest cities of the Netherlands. In 2006, Amsterdam had 743,000 inhabitants and Rotterdam, 589,000. Both metropolises are located in the western part of the country and belong to the Randstad, a densely populated string of cities within a short distance of each other encircling the country's so-called 'Green Heart', a mostly rural and relatively sparsely inhabited area. Amsterdam and Rotterdam are the most significant economic centres in the country, and their economic power is enhanced by the international airport Schiphol being located a short distance from Amsterdam, and by the large Europoort transfer port of Rotterdam. Schiphol and Europoort raise a large share of the national income.

It is precisely these two cities that have attracted many immigrants since the 1960s, more so than elsewhere in or outside the Randstad, although The Hague comes close. Currently, Amsterdam is the world's leading city with regard to the number of different nationalities represented by its inhabitants (about 175).

Turkish and Moroccan migration trends to the two cities are comparable to the ups and downs of the national trends (see Figure 2.3). In general, Amsterdam has attracted more migrants than Rotterdam. And although Amsterdam is home to more Moroccans, Turks have migrated in larger numbers to Rotterdam. In 2006, of all people of Moroccan descent living in the Netherlands, 20.2 per cent lived in Amsterdam and 11.3 per cent in Rotterdam. For people of Turkish descent these percentages are 10.5 for Amsterdam and 12.4 for Rotterdam.

In both cities, the share of migrants (first generation) and migrant descendants (second generation) among the total population is high: 49 per cent in Amsterdam and 46 per cent in Rotterdam. In the Netherlands as a whole, the number is 19 per cent. Among this national per-

Figure 2.3 *Total population (top), Dutch population (bottom) and total number of Turks + Moroccans in Amsterdam and Rotterdam, by age group, absolute numbers, 2006*

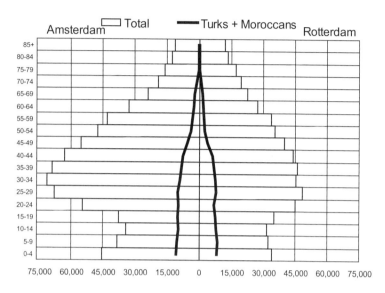

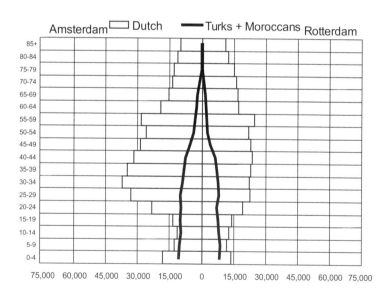

MIGRATION HISTORY AND DEMOGRAPHIC CHARACTERISTICS 33

Figure 2.4 *First- and second-generation Turks (top) and Moroccans (bottom) in Amsterdam and Rotterdam, by age group, absolute numbers, 2006*

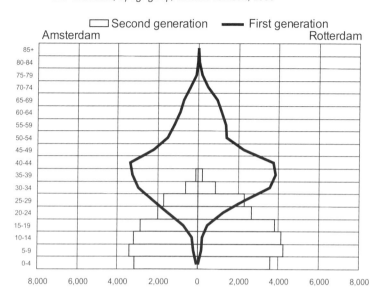

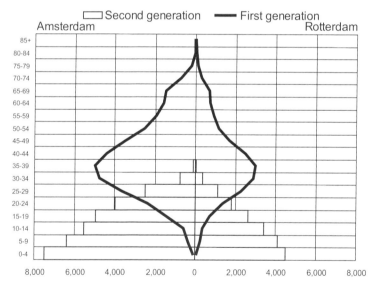

Note: The survey respondents were selected from the darkest bars.

centage, people of Turkish descent form the largest group, then followed by people of Surinamese and Moroccan descent.

Surinamese comprise the largest group in both cities. The population of Moroccan descent is, at 9 per cent, the second largest group in Amsterdam, while people of Turkish descent form 5 per cent of the total Amsterdam population. In Rotterdam, Turks are, at 8 per cent, the second largest group and Moroccans follow closely at 6 per cent.

In both cities and for both groups, the share of first-generation immigrants is still larger than that of the second generation. In 2006, there were 65,400 people of Moroccan descent living in Amsterdam, of which 47 per cent belong to the second generation. The population of Turkish descent in Amsterdam is only half as numerous: 38,300 in total, of which 43 per cent is of the second generation. In Rotterdam, people of Moroccan descent number at 45,200 and those of Turkish descent, at 36,700; the shares of the second generation are 47 per cent and 48 per cent, respectively.

In both Amsterdam and Rotterdam, first-generation Moroccans and Turks are heavily concentrated in age groups of 30 years and upwards; the second generation is concentrated in age groups of up to twenty years (see Figures 2.3 and 2.4). People of Turkish and Moroccan descent form only a small share of the total population, though this is much less the case in the younger age groups. Up to age twenty, about a quarter of the two cities' total population is of Turkish or Moroccan descent; between the ages of twenty and 30, about one in six; between the ages of 30 and 40, one in eight.

2.4 Demographic characteristics of the second generation in the TIES survey

We now turn to a description of the basic demographic characteristics of the TIES survey population. From the previous section, it became apparent that, even though they are only between eighteen and 35 years old, our respondents belong to the second generation's oldest age groups at present. It was noted, furthermore, that Amsterdam is home to more people of Moroccan descent than is Rotterdam, but that Rotterdam is home to more people of Turkish descent than is Amsterdam.

2.4.1 Demographic characteristics of the second generation

The age and sex distribution of the survey population corresponds with that based on official statistical data of Amsterdam and Rotterdam. The second generation is still relatively young: within the survey age range of eighteen to 35, those in their late teens and early twenties (second-

Table 2.1 *Age distribution, by ethnic group and sex in Amsterdam*

	Second generation				Comparison group	
	Turks		Moroccans			
	Men	Women	Men	Women	Men	Women
18-19	13.9	8.3	20.8	17.2	1.9	3.4
20-24	31.8	44.8	43.9	43.0	21.7	22.5
25-29	37.4	31.9	24.1	29.7	32.6	32.2
30-36	16.9	14.9	11.2	10.1	43.7	41.9
Total	100.0	100.0	100.0	100.0	100.0	100.0
Mean age	24.8	24.5	23.4	23.8	28.1	28.0
Standard deviation	4.6	4.3	4.2	4.0	4.6	4.3
N	109	128	119	123	123	136

Table 2.2 *Age distribution, by ethnic group and sex in Rotterdam*

	Second generation				Comparison group	
	Turks		Moroccans			
	Men	Women	Men	Women	Men	Women
18-19	8.4	9.2	31.3	23.9	5.1	7.9
20-24	46.7	37.6	40.5	46.9	21.7	28.1
25-29	29.3	36.8	21.4	17.4	34.4	19.7
30-36	15.6	16.5	6.8	11.8	38.8	44.2
Total	100.0	100.0	100.0	100.0	100.0	100.0
Mean age	24.8	25.4	22.4	23.2	27.7	27.6
Standard deviation	4.3	4.6	3.9	4.3	4.8	5.3
N	133	130	127	124	127	126

generation Moroccans) and those in their twenties (second-generation Turks) form the majority (Tables 2.1 and 2.2). Over the two cities combined, the Moroccan second generation is younger than the Turkish, and both are younger than the comparison group. Second-generation Amsterdam Turks are, at 24.7 years, on average one year older than the second-generation Amsterdam Moroccans, though they are 3.5 years younger than the Amsterdam comparison group. Second-generation Turks in Rotterdam are more than two years older than second-generation Rotterdam Moroccans and only 2.5 years younger than the Rotterdam comparison group.

A large majority of the second-generation Turks and Moroccans – 94 and 93 per cent, respectively – has Dutch nationality (Table 2.3). Among them, many have Turkish or Moroccan citizenship as well. Second-generation Turks more often have such dual nationality than second-generation Moroccans. This result is surprising because, according to Moroccan law, one cannot give up his or her Moroccan nationality. However, it may be possible that, in some cases, parents of second-generation Moroccan respondents did not register their children after

Table 2.3 Citizenship, by ethnic group

	Second generation	
	Turks	Moroccans
Dutch only	35.4	52.2
Dual	58.6	40.4
Turkish or Moroccan only	5.8	6.9
Neither	0.2	0.6
Total	100.0	100.0
N	500	493

Table 2.4 Neighbourhood of residence during early to mid-teens (ages 12-16), by ethnic group

	Second generation		
	Turks	Moroccans	Comparison group
Same as now	57.1	55.6	16.1
Different	42.9	44.4	83.9
Total	100.0	100.0	100.0
N	434	409	470

birth to acquire Moroccan citizenship. Those who do not actually have a Moroccan passport reported single, rather than dual, citizenship. Just over half of second-generation Turks (52 per cent) and Moroccans (57 per cent) indicated that they received Dutch nationality at birth. There are no statistically significant differences by ethnic group and sex. Those who did not receive Dutch nationality at birth were, on average, sixteen to seventeen years old when they naturalised.

Not all second-generation Turks and Moroccans grew up in the same neighbourhood as where they were living at the time of the survey. In general, about four to five out of every ten second-generation Turk or Moroccan lived somewhere else[3] during their early to mid-teenage years (Table 2.4). There are statistically significant differences by ethnic group, though not by sex. Members of the comparison group are considerably more mobile: more than eight out of ten lived somewhere else during their early to mid-teens. In this regard, there is some difference between Rotterdam and Amsterdam, in that Amsterdam is home to a slightly more mobile population.

2.4.2 Demographic characteristics of the parents

In terms of survey eligibility, at least one parent of a second-generation Turkish respondent had to have been born in Turkey and at least one parent of a second-generation Moroccan respondent had to have been born in Morocco, while the requirement for the comparison group was to have had both parents born in the Netherlands. Table 2.5 shows that,

Table 2.5 *Parents' country of birth, by ethnic group*

	Second generation	
	Turks	Moroccans
Both in Turkey/Morocco	96.8	93.9
Father in Turkey/Morocco, mother in the Netherlands	2.5	2.9
Father in the Netherlands, mother in Turkey/Morocco	0.5	1.1
Father in Turkey/Morocco, mother elsewhere	0.0	1.4
Father elsewhere, mother in Turkey/Morocco	0.2	0.7
Total	100.0	100.0
N	500	488

of almost all second-generation respondents, both parents were born in Turkey or Morocco. Just 6 per cent of the Moroccan second generation had a father or mother born in the Netherlands or, in a few cases, another country. For second-generation Turks, the percentage was even lower: a mere 3 per cent has a parent who was born in the Netherlands (in most cases, it was the mother).

Some parents had migrated to the Netherlands at a fairly young age. One of the survey questions pertained to the place where parents had lived the most up until age fifteen. Around 3 per cent of the fathers and 6 per cent of the mothers of both second-generation Turkish and Moroccan respondents were already in the Netherlands at that time of their life. Thus, for this minority of respondents, not only were they themselves socialised and educated in Dutch society, but so was one of their parents.

First-generation Turkish parents mainly originate from five provinces located in the centre of Turkey: Kayseri, Karaman, Sivas, Ankara and Yozgat (Map 2.1). First-generation Turkish fathers in Amsterdam mainly come from Ankara, whereas first-generation Turkish mothers in Am-

Map 2.1 *Main areas of origin of Turkish parents are coloured dark grey.*

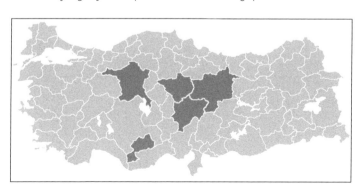

Source: http://en.wikipedia.org/wiki/Turkey

Map 2.2 *Main areas of origin of Moroccan parents are coloured dark grey.*

The two southern-most regions on the map reflect the Western Sahara. Although Morocco recognises the area as its own so-called Southern Provinces, the issue of sovereignty remains internationally disputed.
Source: http://en.wikipedia.org/wiki/Morocco

sterdam come from Ankara and Karaman. First-generation Turkish fathers and mothers in Rotterdam both originate mainly from Kayseri (not statistically significant).

Almost three out of ten first-generation Moroccan parents come from the country's north-east Oriental region. Another approximately 16 per cent originates from Tanger-Tetouan (Morocco's most northern area opposite Gibraltar) or from Taza-Al Hoceïma-Taounate, also in the north (see Map 2.2). First-generation Moroccan parents in Amsterdam originate more often from Tanger, while those in Rotterdam more often from Taza (this fact is statistically significant).

The majority of the fathers arrived in the Netherlands during the period 1965-1974, and most mothers, between 1975 and 1984. The figures in Table 2.6 correlate with overall immigration trends observed for the Netherlands as a whole (see Figure 2.1).

Table 2.6 *Parents' year of immigration, by ethnic group*

	Second generation			
	Turks		Moroccans	
	Mother	Father	Mother	Father
<=1959	0.1	2.1	1.0	4.7
1960-1964	2.3	6.7	2.3	8.7
1965-1969	10.2	18.4	4.8	24.8
1970-1974	24.4	31.0	21.8	25.9
1975-1979	36.9	26.5	33.1	23.9
1980-1984	17.7	11.9	27.2	7.3
>= 1985	8.3	3.4	9.9	4.6
Total	100.0	100.0	100.0	100.0
N	391	394	396	394

Only a few first-generation Turkish and Moroccan fathers have been in the Netherlands for less than twenty years; the majority of them have lived in the country for at least 30 years. Their average duration of residence is about 33 to 34 years, being a little longer for the Moroccans than for the Turks. We can speculate on the reason for this difference, though it is not statistically significant: is it only chance, or have differential emigration rates affected the average duration of residence? The process of family reunification started earlier among Turks than it did among Moroccans, which is still reflected in the slightly lower overall duration of residence of the first-generation Moroccan mothers (28.6 years) when compared to that of first-generation Turkish mothers (29.7 years) (see Table 2.7). Reasons for parents to come to the Netherlands correspond with what is known from the migration literature: three-quarters of both the first-generation Turkish and Moroccan mothers migrated because of marriage or family reunion reasons, while two-thirds of the first-generation Turkish fathers and four-fifths of the Moroccan fathers migrated for work.

What is the current situation of respondents' parents? Already deceased by the time of the survey were about 2 per cent of first-generation Moroccan mothers, 4 per cent of first-generation Turkish mothers and 4 per cent of mothers in the comparison group. Corresponding figures for deceased fathers are as follows: 9 per cent among the Moroccans, 10 percent among the Turks and 10 per cent among the comparison group. The lower survival ratio for the fathers is most likely related to their older age structure: the survey data on parents who are still alive indicate that first-generation Turkish mothers are an average of 50 years old and first-generation Moroccan mothers, 51, while mothers born in the Netherlands, 56. Turkish fathers are an average of 54 years old, Moroccan fathers, 57, and the fathers of the comparison group, 58.

Table 2.7 *Parents' duration of residence in the Netherlands, by ethnic group*

	Second generation			
	Turks		Moroccans	
	Mother	Father	Mother	Father
<=19 years	2.1	1.3	4.2	1.3
20-24 years	16.4	7.3	20.0	6.8
25-29 years	30.1	23.9	32.6	16.9
30-39 years	45.7	51.7	39.2	55.1
>=40 years	5.7	15.8	4.1	20.0
Total	100.0	100.0	100.0	100.0
Mean duration (years)	29.7	32.7	28.6	33.9
Standard deviation	5.6	6.7	6.3	6.6
N	376	362	389	363

The age difference between Moroccan spouses is considerably larger than that of the other two groups. This phenomenon is consistent with what is known from statistics on age differences upon marriage in Morocco and in Turkey. Respondents in the comparison group are twice as likely as second-generation Turks and Moroccans to have parents with an age difference of less than one year or to have a mother who is older than her spouse.

If both parents are still alive, practically all are married: 98 per cent of first-generation Turkish parents, 96 per cent of first-generation Moroccan parents and 95 per cent of the comparison group's parents. About one-third of the parents still only hold the nationality of their country of origin (Table 2.8). Around 60 per cent of parents have dual citizenship. This means that the majority of the parents are also Dutch by nationality. Comparing the parents with their children, we see that holding only Dutch nationality is more common for the second generation. One-third of the Turkish second generation have only Dutch citizenship, as compared to less than 5 per cent of their parents; half of the Moroccan second generation reports having Dutch citizenship only (despite the fact that according to Moroccan law it is not possible to give up Moroccan citizenship), as compared to about 4 per cent of their parents.

The survey also contains indicators of parents' educational level and employment status just before their migration to the Netherlands. Both indicators are based on answers by the second-generation respondents.

More than half of the first-generation Moroccan and Turkish mothers and almost half of these fathers did not attend school or only had primary education (Table 2.9). Mothers, more often than fathers, and Moroccans, more often than Turks, did not attend school at all. Attending only a Koran school was more characteristic of first-generation Moroccans than first-generation Turks.

Having parents who reached a high level of education is rather common among the comparison group – more than a quarter of the mothers of the comparison group and even a larger share of the fathers

Table 2.8 *Parents' citizenship, by ethnic group*

	Second generation			
	Turks		Moroccans	
	Mother	Father	Mother	Father
Both	61.4	59.3	56.9	58.6
Only Dutch	3.8	4.4	4.7	3.3
Only country of origin	32.8	32.6	34.8	32.6
Do not know	1.9	3.7	3.6	5.4
Total	100.0	100.0	100.0	100.0
N	482	494	467	483

Table 2.9 *Parents' (highest) level of education, by ethnic group*

	Second generation				Comparison group	
	Turks		Moroccans			
	Mother	Father	Mother	Father	Mother	Father
Did not attend school	16.8	7.3	39.7	21.2	0.2	0.8
Only attended a Koran school, religious lessons	0.2	0.6	2.1	8.9	0.0	0.0
Primary school	46.9	40.8	20.4	22.7	5.2	6.9
Lower vocational education	7.5	11.2	3.8	4.9	19.1	14.5
Lower general secondary education	11.5	11.2	10.3	6.0	17.6	9.4
Middle vocational education	3.8	10.6	7.1	9.2	22.6	16.5
Higher general secondary education	1.3	2.0	2.0	3.1	6.6	6.4
Tertiary education (Bachelor)	1.5	4.0	0.9	3.0	16.8	20.4
Tertiary education (Master)	1.6	1.8	0.2	0.8	6.4	18.4
Do not know	9.0	10.5	13.5	20.1	5.5	6.6
Total	100.0	100.0	100.0	100.0	100.0	100.0
N	500	500	492	492	512	512

is highly educated. Among first-generation Moroccan and Turkish fathers, this is less than 8 per cent, and the figures are even lower for the mothers.

With respect to parents' employment status before coming to the Netherlands, we see from Table 2.10 that more than half of the first-generation Turkish and Moroccan fathers had a paid job or business. Only 8 per cent of the first-generation Moroccan mothers and 10 per cent of the first-generation Turkish mothers had a job before migrating.

Table 2.11 gives some further information on the father's job vis-à-vis its SBC level (the Dutch standard occupational classification). The majority of both first-generation Turkish and Moroccan fathers had a job at the lower or secondary level. Only 3 per cent of the Turkish fathers and

Table 2.10 *Mother/father worked before migrating to the Netherlands, by ethnic group*

	Second generation			
	Turks		Moroccans	
	Mother	Father	Mother	Father
Yes	10.3	55.8	8.3	62.7
No	84.5	30.5	84.9	19.8
Don't know	5.3	13.7	6.8	17.5
Total	100.0	100.0	100.0	100.0
N	467	472	460	480

Table 2.11 *Occupation of father before migration to the Netherlands, according to SBC* classification, by ethnic group*

	Second generation	
	Turks	Moroccans
Elementary	11.4	8.5
Lower	36.8	35.2
Secondary	33.8	31.2
Higher	2.6	1.5
Scientific	0.4	0.4
Don't know	15.0	23.2
Total	100.0	100.0
N	756	286

*Standaard Beroepenclassificatie 1992

2 per cent of the Moroccan fathers had a job at the higher or scientific level before migrating. It has to be taken into account that 15 per cent of the second-generation Turkish and 23 per cent of the second-generation Moroccan respondents did not know their fathers job before migrating.

2.4.3 Demographic characteristics of the siblings

One-child families are uncommon among the Turkish and Moroccan first-generation parents: less than 3 per cent of the Turkish and Moroccan second-generation respondents report that they do not have any brothers or sisters; across the comparison group, this figure is almost three times as high (8 per cent). Moroccan families are larger than Turkish ones, while the families in the comparison group are the smallest. The Turkish second generation has 3.0 brothers and sisters on average; the Moroccan second generation, 5.2; and the respondents in the comparison group, just 1.6 (Table 2.12).

Table 2.12 *Number of siblings, by ethnic group*

	Second generation		
	Turks	Moroccans	Comparison group
None	1.1	2.3	7.7
1	15.9	3.4	50.8
2	27.8	8.6	25.2
3	27.3	16.7	9.9
4+	27.8	69.0	6.5
Total	100.0	100.0	100.0
Mean	3.0	5.2	1.6
Standard deviation	1.7	2.9	1.2
N	500	493	512

2.4.4 Household size and position

About one-third of the respondents in the comparison group lives alone, while another one-third lives with only one other person in the household. Among the second-generation Turks and Moroccans, three-quarters live in households of at least three persons (Table 2.13). Second-generation Moroccans live in households of five or more other persons more often than second-generation Turks do. There is hardly any difference between Amsterdam and Rotterdam in this respect: in both cities the household size of the Turkish families is, on average, 3.6 persons, while that of the Moroccan families is 4.1. Among the small percentage of second-generation Turks and Moroccans who live alone, there are hardly any women, though slightly more women than men live alone among the comparison group.

The differences found among second-generation Turks and Moroccans and the comparison group may be partially explained by the fact that the comparison group is, on average, a few years older, as well as by the fact that unmarried children in Turkish and Moroccan families are less likely to leave the parental home. When a division is made according to whether respondents have their own household or are still living in the parental household, we see that the latter are much larger than the former. We can also detect (from the number of respondents in Table 2.13) that many more respondents live in their own households than with their parents, and that, among Moroccans, the percentage living with parents is the largest, while it is lowest for the comparison group. This finding is a reflection of the variation in age.

Two-thirds of the Turkish respondents lives in their own households (i.e. not their parents' household) (Table 2.14). This share is still less than that of the comparison group, among whom almost nine out of

Table 2.13 *Household size, by ethnic group and type of household*

	Second generation				Comparison group	
	Turks		Moroccans			
	In own household	In household of origin	In own household	In household of origin	In own household	In household of origin
1	7.0	0.0	17.7	0.0	38.2	0.0
2	20.0	11.3	23.3	7.2	37.5	13.6
3	25.6	18.9	21.4	7.4	15.0	38.1
4	26.9	34.0	16.0	24.0	7.7	32.9
5+	20.4	35.7	21.6	61.5	1.5	15.4
Total	100.0	100.0	100.0	100.0	100.0	100.0
Mean	3.4	4.2	3.2	5.3	2.0	3.5
Standard deviation	1.4	1.4	1.8	1.9	1.0	1.0
N	342	158	277	216	456	56

Table 2.14 *Household composition, by ethnic group and sex*

	Second generation				Comparison group	
	Turks		Moroccans			
	Men	Women	Men	Women	Men	Women
One-person household	6.2	3.7	14.6	5.0	32.3	36.4
Respondent in own household	62.0	68.3	35.2	57.4	56.0	55.5
Respondent in household of parents/grandparents	31.8	27.9	50.2	37.7	11.7	8.1
Total	100.0	100.0	100.0	100.0	100.0	100.0
N	242	258	246	247	250	262

ten are found to be living in their own households. Living in one's own household for Moroccans is nearly as common (46 per cent) as living in the household of one's parents or grandparents (44 per cent). Perhaps the high share of adult children in Moroccan parental households is related to the fact that the Moroccans we surveyed are, on average, younger than the other two groups, and that they tend to marry later than Turks. In any case, living in the parental household is least common among the comparison group. Only for Moroccans are there statistically significant differences between men and women.

Main reasons for leaving the home and living independently differ among the three groups (Table 2.15). Getting married is the most important reason for Turks and, though less so, it remains an important reason for Moroccans. For both Turks and Moroccans, differences by sex were statistically significant; women were more likely to leave the parental home for reasons of marriage than men. The most important reason for Moroccan men to leave the parental home was to live independently. In the comparison group, pursuing studies was the most important reason

Table 2.15 *Reasons for leaving the parental home in %, by ethnic group*

	Second generation		Comparison group
	Turks	Moroccans	
Marriage	38.2	19.9	1.6
Living together	8.2	6.9	15.9
Live independently	22.5	28.1	23.1
Study	13.2	21.3	52.7
Work	3.4	3.1	4.4
Parents went back to country of origin	3.0	1.4	n.a.
Problems with parents	10.8	6.3	4.5
Other	8.3	20.0	4.6
N	350	300	456

Note: Percentages do not add up to 100 because respondents could give more than one reason.

to leave home. This last figure may be inflated, given that Amsterdam and Rotterdam are both important centres for higher education. Nevertheless, among the comparison group, leaving the parental home for education purposes was more common than leaving in order to cohabit (as opposed to get married), which came in at second place, and leaving to live independently, which came in at third place. Only for the comparison group did we find statistically significant sex differences for living together; comparison group women were more likely to leave the parental home to live together than their male counterparts. Pursuing studies was the third most important reason for Turks; Turkish men were (statistically) more likely to leave the parental home for study than Turkish women.

2.5 Conclusions

The immigration history of the Turkish and the Moroccan populations dates back to the mid-1960s. Apart from the Surinamese, these two groups form the largest populations of foreign descent in the Netherlands. The country's two major cities of Amsterdam and Rotterdam have attracted big shares of both groups, with Moroccans being the more dominant in Amsterdam and Turks in Rotterdam. The first generation is still larger than the second generation, but the latter is increasing rapidly, relative to the former. One in four Amsterdam and Rotterdam residents below twenty years old is of Turkish or Moroccan descent, frequently being a member of the second generation. As family reunification took place basically between the mid-1970s and the mid-1980s, the second generation is still young on average, and this is reflected in the mean age of our survey population (age group 18-35 years): the Moroccans are, on average, 23.3 years old, the Turks, 24.9, while the comparison group, at 27.9, is oldest. A large majority of the second generation has Dutch citizenship – about half of them have held it since birth – and quite often they hold dual citizenship. In this respect, they differ from their parents, about one-third of whom still does not have Dutch citizenship.

Most of the second generation's fathers migrated to the Netherlands in the period 1965-1974, and most of the mothers in the years 1975-1984, overwhelmingly because of work (for fathers) or family reunification (for mothers). Very few respondents are of 'mixed' origin, i.e. having one parent who was born in the Netherlands. Moroccan parents largely originate from northern and north-eastern Morocco, Turkish parents originate from central Anatolia, the Asian mainland of Turkey.

A large minority of Moroccans still live at home with their parents, while the comparison group is most likely to live alone or in their own household. Turks take a middle position. The age difference between the three groups certainly informs some of the explanation, but so do the cultural values attached to leaving home: Turks and Moroccans, especially females, tend to live with their parents until they get married, while it is quite common for comparison group respondents to leave the parental household upon high school graduation. This latter fact also explains the relatively high shares of young comparison group members living alone.

Notes

1 This section draws on papers by Choenni (2000) and Bruquetas-Callejo et al. (2007) as well as publications by the Netherlands Social and Cultural Planning Office, e.g. Dagevos & Gijsberts (2007).
2 These individuals were entered into the statistical system as though they were new immigrants in the year of the regularisation.
3 Just a few respondents indicated that they lived in Turkey or Morocco during their early to mid-teens. They were listed in the survey as belonging to the second generation because of eligibility on other grounds.

References

Amersfoort, J.M.M. van (1986), 'Nederland als immigratieland', in L. van den Berg-Eldering (ed.), *Van gastarbeider tot immigrant. Marokkanen en Turken in Nederland, 1965-1985*, 15-46. Alphen aan den Rijn: Samson.

Bruquetas-Callejo, M., B. Garcés-Mascareñas, R. Penninx & P. Scholten (2007), *Policymaking related to immigration and integration. The Dutch Case*. IMISCOE Working Paper No. 15.

Butter, E. (2000), *Turken in Nederland*. ACB Kenniscentrum, www.acbkenniscentrum.nl/turken.

Choenni, C. (2000), 'Ontwikkelingen van het rijksoverheidsbeleid voor etnische minderheden 1977-2000', in N. van Nimwegen & G. Beets (eds.), *Bevolkingsvraagstukken in Nederland anno 2000. Werkverband Periodieke Rapportage Bevolkingsvraagstukken*. NIDI rapport # 58:131-144. The Hague: NIDI.

Dagevos, J. & M. Gijsberts (eds.) (2007), *Jaarrapport integratie 2007*. The Hague: Sociaal en Cultureel Planbureau (SCP-publicatie; 2007-27).

Groenendijk, K. (2004), 'Legal concepts of integration in EU migration law', *European Journal of Migration and Law* 6(2): 111-126.

Ministerie van Binnenlandse Zaken (1983), *Minderhedenbeleid*. Tweede Kamer 1982-1983, 16102, nos. 20-21. The Hague.

Nicolaas, H. & A. Sprangers (2000), 'De nieuwe gastarbeider', *CBS Index* 8: 26-28.

Nicolaas, H., A. Sprangers & H. Witvliet (2003), 'Arbeidsmigranten en hun gezinnen', *Bevolkingstrends CBS*, second quarter: 20-23.

Oers, R. van, B. de Hart & K. Groenendijk (2006), 'Netherlands'. In: R. Bauböck, E. Ersbøll, K. Groenendijk & H. Waldrauch (eds.), *Acquisition and Loss of Nationality. Policies and Trends in 15 European States. Volume 2: Country analyses*, 391-434. Amsterdam: Amsterdam University Press.

Wetenschappelijke Raad voor het Regeringsbeleid (1979), *Etnische Minderheden*, Rapporten aan de Regering no. 17. The Hague: Staatsuitgeverij.
Wetenschappelijke Raad voor het Regeringsbeleid (1989), *Allochtonenbeleid*, Rapporten aan de Regering no. 36. The Hague: SDU.
Wissen, L. van & J. de Beer (2000), 'Internationale migratie in Nederland: trends, achtergronden, motieven en vooruitzichten', in N. van Nimwegen & G. Beets (eds.), *Bevolkingsvraagstukken in Nederland anno 2000*. Werkverband Periodieke Rapportage Bevolkingsvraagstukken, 147-172. The Hague: NIDI.

3 Housing and segregation

Carlo van Praag and Jeannette Schoorl

3.1 Introduction

Housing is a basic necessity but also a scarce and expensive commodity. For these reasons, in many countries public authorities do not leave the distribution of housing entirely to the free market, but intervene in favour of the low-income groups who find it difficult or impossible to find decent accommodation on their own. In the present chapter, we will first look at the housing situation of people of Turkish and Moroccan descent in Amsterdam and Rotterdam (section 3.2), as well as at issues of segregation and concentration in the two cities (section 3.3). Housing policies will be discussed in section 3.4. We will then look in more detail at the housing situation of the second generation in Amsterdam and Rotterdam (section 3.5), in comparison with the contextual data presented in the earlier sections of this chapter.

3.2 Housing situation

In the Netherlands, government intervention in the housing sector used to be especially strong, and gave rise to an extensive and very complex system of measures involving many parties of the rental housing market and affecting the majority of consumers. While the system was mostly abolished in the 1990s, the Dutch housing market still clearly shows remnants of the system. It boasts a relatively large rental sector (44 per cent of the total housing stock), which is dominated by public housing (34 per cent of the total housing stock) in the big cities. Notably in Amsterdam and Rotterdam, these features stand out all the more. The majority of the dwellings there are part of the public rental sector. Both cities are, moreover, characterised by the relative absence of single-family dwellings and the dominance of small flats and the comparatively large proportion of older housing (Table 3.1).

While public interference with housing has significantly decreased over the past decades, some major facilities are still in operation and deserve mention. A large part of the rental sector is still subject to price control, and many tenants pay probably less than the market price.

Table 3.1 *Some characteristics of the housing stock, 2004 (all figures in % of total housing stock)*

	Rental sector	Public housing sector	Single-family dwellings	Flats of less than 4 rooms	Built before 1960
Amsterdam	80	53	15	62	59
Rotterdam	71	55	27	45	48
The Netherlands	44	34	71	20	33

Source: www.grotevier.nl

One-third of the tenants also profit from individual rent relief. What's more, house owners can deduct the interest paid on their mortgage from their taxable income.

As demonstrated by Table 3.1, the housing corporations own more than half of the dwelling stock in Amsterdam and Rotterdam. Owner-occupancy does not occur nearly as much with Turks and Moroccans as with the comparison group. It is on the rise, however (SCP/WODC/CBS 2005). Outside the two cities the chance of owner-occupancy among people of Turkish or Moroccan descent is nearly twice as high as within.

Right from the start, the population of Turkish and Moroccan descent has been lagging behind the rest of the population, no doubt because of their relatively low incomes and their concentration in the big cities. In the past, discrimination in the housing market, by private landlords as well as public housing corporations, also contributed to these arrears. Over the last two decades, the gap has narrowed to some extent (SCP/WODC/CBS 2005). Data displayed in Table 3.2 are derived from the national WoOn survey (2006) on the housing situation in the Netherlands undertaken in 2006. Though the sample was rather large (64,000 respondents), it was still too small to shed sufficient light on the housing situation of particular ethnic groups, such as Turks or Moroccans, in either Amsterdam or Rotterdam. However, when the two ethnic groups and the two cities were taken together, the number of cases was sufficiently large to permit the presentation of some basic results.

It becomes clear from Table 3.2 that a greater proportion of Turks or Moroccans occupy flats or apartments than do members of the comparison group. On the whole, the former's housing situation is less favourable. Their dwellings are smaller than those of the comparison group and date more often from the 1950s and 1960s, which implies that they are of lower quality (not yet having been subjected to urban renewal) than pre-war housing. Turks and Moroccans are less often to be found in houses built in more recent periods. Because of their larger households and the fewer rooms available, the average number of persons per room stands at 1.0, whereas it is only 0.71 for the comparison group.

Table 3.2 *Dwelling characteristics of ethnic groups in Amsterdam, Rotterdam and the Netherlands (in % unless otherwise stated)*

	Dutch in Amsterdam/ Rotterdam	Turks/Moroccans in Amsterdam/ Rotterdam	Turks/Moroccans in the Netherlands
Type of dwelling			
Single-family dwellings	35.9	11.5	45.3
Flats/apartment complexes	64.1	88.5	54.7
Building period			
Before 1945	36.1	29.5	16.3
1945-1959	10.2	18.3	17.4
1959-1969	9.6	10.8	18.6
1970-1979	9.3	6.9	16.1
1980-1989	15.3	19.6	16.2
1990-1999	15.3	11.9	11.0
2000 or later	4.1	3.1	4.3
Average number of rooms	3.90	3.72	4.02
Surface available (m^2)			
Living room	32.4	24.4	27.4
Total dwelling	101.7	74.7	93.1

Source: WoON 2006

Table 3.3 shows that the overwhelming majority of Turks or Moroccans, both in the two big cities and in the country as a whole, are part of the public rental sector. A much smaller though still sizable share of the Dutch big-city dwellers also rents from a public housing corporation. As has been demonstrated by Table 3.1, these corporations own more than half of the dwelling stock in Amsterdam and Rotterdam. Owner-occupancy does not occur nearly as much with Turks or Moroccans as

Table 3.3 *Ownership and rent levels of the Turkish/Moroccan and Dutch populations (in multiple-person households)*

	Dutch in Amsterdam/ Rotterdam	Turks/Moroccans in Amsterdam/ Rotterdam	Turks/Moroccans in the Netherlands
Ownership (%)			
Owner-occupied	38.6	12.1	23.5
Public rental sector	42.9	79.9	72.0
Private rental sector	18.5	8.0	4.5
Rent and rent subsidy			
Gross rent (€ per month)	451	379	401
Average rent subsidy for all tenants (€ per month)	24	69	67
Net rent (€ per month)	427	310	334
Per cent of tenants receiving rent subsidy	16.7	44.6	41.5

Source: WoON 2006

with the comparison group. It is on the rise, however (SCP/WODC/ CBS 2005). Outside the two cities the chance of owner-occupancy among Turks or Moroccans is nearly twice as high as within.

Though Turks or Moroccans pay lower gross rents than the comparison group, they are eligible for rent subsidy far more often on account of their lower incomes. As a result, the average net rent they pay lies considerably under the level of the comparison group.

3.3 Concentration and segregation

In both cities, slightly over 14 per cent of the population is of either Moroccan or Turkish descent. They are unevenly spread out over the city. While in many neighbourhoods both groups taken together do not exceed 5 per cent of the population, in other neighbourhoods, 30 per cent and over are found (see Maps 3.1 and 3.2). In one Amsterdam neighbourhood, no less than two-thirds of the population is either of Moroccan or Turkish descent.

In Rotterdam, the areas in which Moroccans and Turks are concentrated still follow the same pattern as that discerned in the 1920s by Park and Burgess of the Chicago School in sociology. These areas, situated in a concentric zone (the so-called zone in transition) around the central business district, are struck by urban blight and offer the cheapest and

Map 3.1 *Population of Turkish and Moroccan descent as a percentage of the total population in postal code areas of Amsterdam, 1 January 2007*

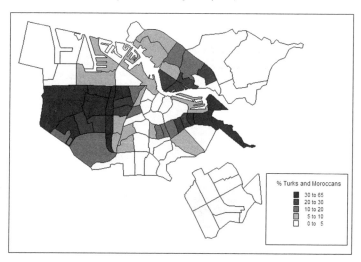

Source: GBA Amsterdam

Map 3.2 *Population of Turkish and Moroccan descent as a percentage of the total population in postal code areas of Rotterdam, 1 January 2007*

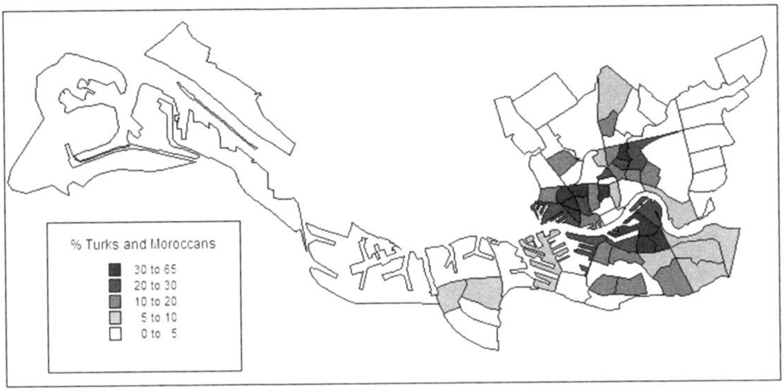

[Map showing % Turks and Moroccans by postal code area, with legend: 30 to 65, 20 to 30, 10 to 20, 5 to 10, 0 to 5]

Source: GBA Rotterdam

the worst available housing. In the present situation, urban blight is hardly a factor anymore, though it can still be maintained that the bottom of the housing market is, as before, to be found in the neighbourhoods around the central business district. Originally, Amsterdam presented a similar picture, with relative concentrations of Moroccan and Turkish neighbourhoods around the city centre during the nineteenth and early twentieth centuries. Though remnants of this pattern are still discernable, the overall picture has become quite different. Moroccans and Turks show a massive concentration in the post-war neighbourhoods in the west of the town and more recently, in the north. These neighbourhoods date mainly from the 1950s and 1960s and are dominated by the public rental sector. The pre-war neighbourhoods have become increasingly popular with young urban professionals and have undergone significant gentrification. Many dwellings there are now owner-occupied. As a result, the bottom of the housing market has shifted to more recent neighbourhoods farther away from the city centre.

Turks and Moroccans live mostly in the same neighbourhoods. Their mutual segregation (as expressed by the index of dissimilarity) is only 10.6 in Amsterdam and 16.7 in Rotterdam. The corresponding coefficients of correlation are 0.97 and 0.87, respectively. The neighbourhoods in which the two groups are concentrated often have non-western majorities. In the 36 neighbourhoods with more than 20 per cent Moroccans or Turks in their population, 24 have non-western majorities. All of the eighteen neighbourhoods where more than 30 per cent of the population is of Moroccan or Turkish descent have non-western majorities. Maps 3.1 and 3.2 suggest a certain level of segregation of the two groups from the rest of the population and from the comparison group population in particular. Table 3.4 can only confirm this assumption.

Table 3.4 *Segregation of Turks and Moroccans in Amsterdam and Rotterdam, 1 January 2007*

	% of total population in neighbourhoods where 1/4 of the ethnic group is concentrated	% of total population in neighbourhoods where 1/2 of the ethnic group is concentrated	Segregation from rest of the population (index of segregation)	Segregation from native Dutch (index of dissimilarity)
Amsterdam				
Moroccans	11.5	22.0	40.6	44.8
Turks	8.0	18.9	43.6	49.2
Rotterdam				
Moroccans	10.9	22.6	39.3	51.8
Turks	8.0	19.7	41.8	53.4

Source: Statistics Netherlands

In Amsterdam, a quarter of the Moroccans reside in a number of neighbourhoods where only 11.5 per cent of the total population is settled, and half of them are concentrated in an area that lodges no more than 22 per cent of the total population. If the distributions of Moroccans and the rest of the population are compared in their totality, the index of segregation that can be computed stands at 40.6.

The Turks and Moroccans are among the most segregated groups of the population. Indices of segregation in both cities for the total population of non-western descent (including Turks and Moroccans) amount to 37 (not in Table 3.4).

3.4 Housing policies

Unlike asylum seekers, ethnic groups do not form special target groups in housing policy. As a result of their comparatively modest incomes and their concentration in the big cities, Turks and Moroccans are overrepresented in the public housing sector.

The main focus of concern in the two cities has been and still is the concentration of immigrants in certain neighbourhoods. In the past, the local authorities in several cities made attempts in the direction of a dispersal policy, essentially by influencing the housing allocation in such a way that the growth of the ethnic minorities would be curbed in districts where they were concentrated, while at the same time entry into other areas would be promoted.

The prime protagonist was the city of Rotterdam which, as early as 1972, wanted to link the allocation of housing to the ethnic composition of the neighbourhoods. The programme was annulled by the state as being discriminatory. Again, in 1979, Rotterdam came up with a similar proposal, which was likewise aborted on account of fierce opposition from welfare and immigrant organisations. In later years, attention shifted from the ethnic composition of specific neighbourhoods to the ethnic composition of the city as a whole. The local authorities in Rotterdam showed a growing concern about the influx of non-western immigrants and the simultaneous suburbanisation of more prosperous comparison group members with impoverishment of the city as a result. In 2003, the Council adopted a proposal to adapt the Huisvestingswet (Housing Act) in such a way that it could be used to restrict the right of settlement in certain districts of Rotterdam to those with incomes above a certain level. In effect, the measure was directed at non-western immigrants. This time the national government went along with the Rotterdam authorities, and from 2006 on, the new policy was officially applied. It is yet too early to assess the effects of this policy on the composition of the Rotterdam population, but they cannot be very strong, because only a very limited area of the city is involved (Gijsberts & Dagevos 2007: 56-59).

Rotterdam has certainly been the most prominent supporter of a dispersal policy, but not the only one. Several other municipalities have been practising dispersal policies without officially announcing them. Housing corporations frequently maintained a dispersal policy at the micro-level, aimed at distributing immigrants in a certain way along streets and blocks (Penninx et al. 1993: 155-157). Moreover, numerous examples can be given of measures intended at keeping the migrants out of white neighbourhoods, thus increasing their level of concentration in other parts of the city.

In the 1970s and 1980s, large-scale urban renewal programmes were carried out to improve at least the physical environment in the old neighbourhoods, but better housing did not alter the fact that most old neighbourhoods remained close to the bottom of the housing market. Urban renewal was followed in later years by several programmes aimed at improving the social and economic situation of the inhabitants. In 1994, with the introduction of the policy for large cities known as the '*grotestedenbeleid*', the attention shifted from the old neighbourhoods to the city as a whole.

Within the frame of the *grotestedenbeleid* special attention was given to 56 'priority neighbourhoods'. Because of the wide geographical scope of the *grotestedenbeleid*, most of these neighbourhoods were to be found in comparably small towns. With the installation of a new Cabinet in 2007, the focus has been narrowed to 40 of the most problematic urban areas. All in all, 80 postal districts are involved in this programme, of which no less than 41 are located in either Amsterdam or Rotterdam (Bijl et al. 2007: 263–269). Almost without exception, these are the neighbourhoods with the highest concentrations of non-western ethnic inhabitants, especially Moroccans and Turks.

3.5 Housing situation of the second generation

After having sketched the housing situation of the Turkish and Moroccan population in Amsterdam and Rotterdam, we now turn to that of the Turkish and Moroccan second generation in the TIES survey. As our survey group is between eighteen and 35 years old, some of them are still living with their parents (see the previous chapter) and, in that respect, their housing characteristics reflect those of the first generation. Others live alone, having left their parents' home, though they are not, or not yet, living with a partner or a family of their own. Housing requirements for the three groups differ. Table 3.5 provides an overview of the various living arrangements. It is striking that more than one-third of the comparison group lives alone, while almost 30 per cent of the young second-generation Turks and well over 40 per cent of the young second-generation Moroccans continue to live with their parents.

In this chapter we will limit ourselves to an analysis of two groups only: those living with their parents and/or grandparent(s) and those living in a household of their own – mostly as a couple though, in some cases, as a single-parent family or in other types of household (often siblings living together or other relatives or friends). Single-person households are therefore excluded: there are very few such households among the Turkish and Moroccan second generation and, because of the difference in housing situation and housing requirements, single-

Table 3.5 *Household composition, by ethnic group and sex*

	Second generation				Comparison group	
	Turks		Moroccans			
	Men	Women	Men	Women	Men	Women
One-person household	6.1	3.4	14.4	4.8	32.2	36.5
Respondent in own household	62.2	68.6	35.6	57.3	56.1	55.4
Couple without children	12.2	13.5	6.7	8.3	32.0	26.1
Couple with children	20.7	32.6	6.7	17.9	12.8	17.9
Couple with children and Others	7.3	3.4	0.0	1.2	0.7	0.3
Couple with others	3.7	2.2	1.1	2.4	0.5	0.5
Single parent with children	0.0	3.4	0.0	3.6	0.0	4.6
Single parent with children and others	2.4	3.4	4.4	6.0	0.0	0.7
Other households	15.9	10.1	16.7	17.9	10.1	5.3
Respondent in household of origin	31.7	28.1	50.0	38.1	11.7	8.2
In parental household	30.5	27.0	50.0	38.1	11.2	8.2
In grandparental household	1.2	1.1	0.0	0.0	0.5	0.0
Total	100.0	100.0	100.0	100.0	100.0	100.0
N	242	258	246	247	250	262

person households cannot conveniently be grouped together with either of the other categories.

While only a few of the first-generation Turks and Moroccans are home-owners, the second generation who have left the parental home are somewhat more prosperous: over one in four second-generation Turks is an owner-occupier (Table 3.6). They still lag behind the 39 per cent of the comparison group, however, and this applies even more to the Moroccans (14 per cent owner-occupiers). Nevertheless, the difference from the first generation is remarkable.

A large majority of all respondents lives in apartments and, in this respect, there is no difference between the second generation and the comparison group who have left their parents' home (Table 3.7). Second-generation Turks and Moroccans living with their parents are also mostly in apartments, but the comparison group is clearly more well-off: their parents are much more likely to live in single-family or in detached or semi-detached dwellings.

The fact that members of the comparison group still living with their parents are better-off is reconfirmed by other housing characteristics. The houses most of them live in were built between the two world wars and are generally larger and of better-quality construction than the dwellings built in the period after World War II (Table 3.8).

The homes of their parents are generally larger and have more rooms (Table 3.9). The difference between the comparison group and second-generation Turks and Moroccans disappears for those who have set up a family for themselves. However, this is partly a spurious effect, as the household sizes of second-generation Turks and especially second-

Table 3.6 *Home ownership and rental structure, by living arrangement and ethnic group*

	Second generation		Comparison group
	Turks	Moroccans	
In parental/grandparental household			
Owner-occupied	2.3	3.3	28.7
Owner-occupied by parents/parents-in-law	4.7	1.6	14.9
Public rental sector	81.4	91.8	49.5
Private rental sector	11.7	3.3	6.9
Total	100.0	100.0	100.0
N	132	175	49
Own household			
Owner-occupied	25.5	13.4	38.9
Owner-occupied by parents/parents-in-law	7.1	4.5	2.3
Public rental sector	60.2	68.7	30.7
Private rental sector	7.1	13.4	28.1
Total	100.0	100.0	100.0
N	271	198	247

Table 3.7 *Type of dwelling, by living arrangement and ethnic group*

	Second generation		Comparison group
	Turks	Moroccans	
In parental/grandparental household			
Apartment	81.0	82.0	45.1
Single-family dwelling	16.7	18.0	47.1
Semi-detached/detached dwelling	2.4	0.0	6.9
Other	0.0	0.0	1.0
Total	100.0	100.0	100.0
N	132	176	50
Own household			
Apartment	75.5	78.3	77.4
Single-family dwelling	20.6	18.8	16.1
Semi-detached/detached dwelling	1.0	0.0	0.8
Other	3.0	2.8	5.6
Total	100.0	100.0	100.0
N	280	203	261

Table 3.8 *Construction period of dwellings, by living arrangement and ethnic group*

	Second generation		Comparison group
	Turks	Moroccans	
In parental/grandparental household			
Before 1915	6.7	2.0	2.1
1915-1949	13.3	16.3	22.9
1950-1979	36.7	44.9	31.3
1980-2001	33.3	32.7	39.6
2002 or later	10.0	4.1	4.2
Total	100.0	100.0	100.0
N[a]	100	140	47
Own household			
Before 1915	0.0	3.9	11.6
1915-1949	19.2	17.6	38.0
1950-1979	39.7	47.1	27.0
1980-2001	30.1	25.5	17.0
2002 or later	11.0	5.9	6.4
Total	100.0	100.0	100.0
N[b]	207	160	227

[a] There were a fairly large number of respondents who could not estimate the period in which their house was built: 28.6, 18.3 and 5.0 per cent among Turks, Moroccans and the comparison group, respectively.

[b] There were a fairly large number of respondents who could not estimate the period in which their house was built: 25.5, 22.7 and 7.9 per cent among Turks, Moroccans and the comparison group, respectively.

Table 3.9 *Living arrangements and housing characteristics, by ethnic group*

	Second generation		Comparison group
	Turks	Moroccans	
In parental/grandparental household			
Average number of rooms	4.1	4.3	4.6
Average dwelling surface (m^2)	80.0	83.7	116.9
Average number of years in current dwelling	12.4	12.8	13.5
Own household			
Average number of rooms	3.5	3.4	3.3
Average dwelling surface (m^2)	76.3	83.6	80.7
Average number of years in current dwelling	5.2	4.6	3.3

generation Moroccans are somewhat larger, and they, on average, thus have less space per person than the comparison group.

Six out of ten second-generation Turks and Moroccans living with their parents live in a neighbourhood where at least 30 per cent of the population is of Turkish or Moroccan origin. For the second generation living in a household of their own, well over half still live in such neighbourhoods (Table 3.10).

Although a majority of the second generation is satisfied with the ethnic composition in their current neighbourhood, about one-third indicates they would rather live in a neighbourhood with fewer other residents of the same ethnic group. For the comparison group, it is the opposite: they prefer a neighbourhood with more of their own kind (Table 3.11).

These preferences, not unexpectedly, are influenced by the type of neighbourhood one is living in: those residing in neighbourhoods where at least 20 per cent of the population is of Turkish or Moroccan origin are considerably more likely to prefer fewer other residents of the same ethnic group than those already living in less segregated environments (Table 3.12).

Table 3.10 *Degree of neighbourhood concentration,[*] by living arrangement and ethnic group*

	Second generation		Comparison group
	Turks	Moroccans	
In parental/grandparental household			
% living in neighbourhoods with at least 30 % Turks or Moroccans	59.6	59.7	20.2
N	158	216	56
Own household			
% living in neighbourhoods with at least 30 % Turks or Moroccans	53.1	55.6	25.2
N	312	229	276

[*] Turks and Moroccans as a percentage of the total population in postal code areas

Table 3.11 *Living arrangements and neighbourhood preferences, by ethnic group*

	Second generation		Comparison group
	Turks	Moroccans	
In parental/grandparental household			
Prefers same type of neighbourhood	50.0	65.5	42.2
Prefers neighbourhood with lower % of own ethnic group	42.9	29.3	18.6
Prefers neighbourhood with higher % of own ethnic group	7.1	5.2	39.2
Total	100.0	100.0	100.0
N	260	199	256
Own household			
Prefers same type of neighbourhood	57.9	54.4	45.0
Prefers neighbourhood with lower % of own ethnic group	31.6	32.4	7.3
Prefers neighbourhood with higher % of own ethnic group	10.5	13.2	47.7
Total	100.0	100.0	100.0
N	128	169	50

Table 3.12 *Actual and preferred prevalence level of own ethnic group members in neighbourhood, by ethnic group*

	Second generation		Comparison group
	Turks	Moroccans	
At least 20 per cent Turkish/Moroccan population			
Prefers same type of neighbourhood	52.5	58.2	33.0
Prefers neighbourhood with lower % of own ethnic group	39.6	33.7	5.7
Prefers neighbourhood with higher % of own ethnic group	7.9	8.2	61.3
Total	100.0	100.0	100.0
N	230	233	160
Less than 20 per cent Turkish/Moroccan pop.			
Prefers same type of neighbourhood	63.9	60.0	53.1
Prefers neighbourhood with lower % of own ethnic group	22.2	23.3	11.2
Prefers neighbourhood with higher % of own ethnic group	13.9	16.7	35.7
Total	100.0	100.0	100.0
N	158	135	146

There is, perhaps surprisingly, little general difference among the three ethnic groups in their feelings about their neighbourhoods. The sense of social attachment is relatively strong, but decidedly less so among those with a household of their own than among those living with their parents (Table 3.13). In any case, the differences between the ethnic groups are statistically significant for only two of the items.

Duration of residence in the neighbourhood may influence this outcome: those in households of their own average have been in their current dwelling no more than 3.3 years (comparison group) or up to 5.2 years (second-generation Turks), while the average residence duration of those living in their parental home is about thirteen years. Roughly one-third feels negative to very negative about physical aspects of their neighbourhood, such as garbage lying about and the occurrence of crime. Less than one in three residents would agree with the statement that there is hardly any vandalism in their neighbourhood.

Table 3.13 *Percentage agreeing or strongly agreeing with statement on the quality of life in the neighbourhoods, by living arrangement and ethnic group*

	Second generation		Comparison group
	Turks	Moroccans	
In parental/grandparental household			
I feel attached to this neighbourhood	62.8	72.6	65.7
I have good contact with my immediate neighbours	65.0	70.5	72.5
People in this neighbourhood hardly know each other*	14.6	8.3	27.5
There is a lot of garbage lying about in the streets of this neighbourhood	34.1	18.0	30.4
There is a lot of crime in this neighbourhood	34.1	32.8	38.2
There is hardly any vandalism in this neighbourhood	31.0	30.6	20.6
I expect the quality of life in this neighbourhood will deteriorate next year	41.5	19.4	29.4
There aren't enough good schools in this neighbourhood	31.7	27.9	22.5
Own household			
I feel attached to this neighbourhood	48.5	53.5	51.2
I have good contact with my immediate neighbours	60.8	62.3	65.4
People in this neighbourhood hardly know each other	28.7	25.7	33.1
There is a lot of garbage lying about in the streets of this neighbourhood	34.3	29.6	34.2
There is a lot of crime in this neighbourhood	29.7	31.9	29.8
There is hardly any vandalism in this neighbourhood	34.3	32.9	27.6
I expect the quality of life in this neighbourhood will deteriorate next year*	30.0	24.6	14.9
There aren't enough good schools in this neighbourhood	31.0	24.2	18.2

* Differences between groups statistically significant (Kruskal Wallis measure ≤ .001)

3.6 Conclusions

In both cities, Moroccans and Turks form sizable minorities. Taken together, they make up 14 per cent of the total population in both cities. They are not evenly spread out, but rather, concentrated in parts of the city that have lost favour with the rest of the population. Moroccans and Turks largely occupy the same neighbourhoods. In quite a lot of these neighbourhoods, they constitute more than one-fifth – and often, even more than one-third – of the total population. This implies a certain amount of segregation from the rest of the population. In both cities, roughly half of the population of Turkish and Moroccan descent is concentrated in a number of neighbourhoods that house only about a fifth of the total population.

All these observations apply more or less to both the first and the second generations. One has to keep in mind that the second generation for both city populations is still young and consists of about 75 per cent of children living with their parents. Moreover, members of the second generation with their own established households are mostly young adults who have only recently entered the housing market and probably lack the means to move out of their parents' neighbourhoods even if they wish to do so.

Nevertheless, some differences between the generations could be observed. The second generation occupies single-family dwellings somewhat more often than the first. Owner-occupancy was more prevalent in the Turkish second generation than the first, though they still lag far behind the comparison group members. The Turkish second generation, though not the Moroccan second generation, could be found somewhat more often in neighbourhoods dating from the 1980s and later. The TIES data did not provide information on members of either generation who had moved out of the city altogether.

References

Bijl, R., J. Boelhouwer & E. Pommer (eds.) (2007), *De sociale staat van Nederland*. The Hague: Sociaal en Cultureel Planbureau.
Gijsberts, M. & J. Dagevos (2007), *Interventies voor Integratie. Het tegengaan van etnische concentratie en bevorderen van interetnisch contact*. The Hague: Sociaal en Cultureel Planbureau.
Penninx, R., J. Schoorl & C. van Praag (1993), *Consequences of international migration for the receiving countries: The case of the Netherlands*. Amsterdam: Swets and Zeitlinger.
SCP/WODC/CBS (2005), *Jaarrapport integratie 2005*. The Hague.
WoON (2006), WoonOnderzoek Nederland, basismodule Woningmarkt.

4 Education

Helga de Valk and Maurice Crul

4.1 Introduction

Education is of crucial importance in the lives of young adults. Attending school is not only a major part of everyday life, but education is a decisive factor for the future. In literature, educational attainment has been tied to a host of outcomes in adult life. Education is perceived as the key for social mobility. This applies to all children, of course, but may be of even more importance for second-generation youth.

Educational success is related to the opportunities and chances in the educational system as such, but it also has a correlation with the individual characteristics of students and their parents. So, how are second-generation young adults doing in school? What educational experiences do they have in primary and secondary education? What characterises their school career? How well-off are second-generation youth compared with Dutch students? Previous studies often take final outcomes as their subject of research. In this chapter, we take a more dynamic perspective and give insights into the different stages of the educational career of second-generation Turkish and Moroccan young adults and those of the comparison group. Besides the achievements in primary and secondary education, we also pay attention to young adults' experiences in school and the relationship between education and the parental home. We will give an overview of the rich data on education that the TIES survey provides.

4.2 The educational system in the Netherlands

One of the pillars of the Dutch educational system is the freedom to choose a school according to one's own preferences, be they religious or ideological. All schools in the Netherlands, including those that are religious, are state-funded. A pupil is officially expected to enter primary school when he or she turns four years old. Primary school consists of eight grades, so children usually leave at age twelve. At the end of primary school, all children must take a national examination that is crucial for their further school career in secondary school. On the basis of this test result and the recommendation made by their teacher, they will be assigned to follow a specific track in the secondary school system.

Figure 4.1 summarises the current educational system in the Netherlands and provides an overview of the many ways to navigate it. Lower vocational education (vbo)[1] is the lowest stream of secondary education, where children with the lowest recommendation from primary school are placed. Children with a lower general secondary education (mavo or vmbo-t)[2] recommendation or higher usually go to comprehensive schools that include one stream of preparatory middle vocational education (mavo or vmbo-t) and two streams preparing children for tertiary education (havo or vwo).[3] In the first one or two years of comprehensive school, children with different school recommendations study together in what are considered intermediary classes. However, most comprehensive schools (especially since after 2000) have begun to exclusively group together children with similar primary school recommendations. Pupils with a havo diploma can continue on to higher vocational education, while pupils with a vwo diploma usually continue on to university.

Figure 4.1 *The Dutch educational system*

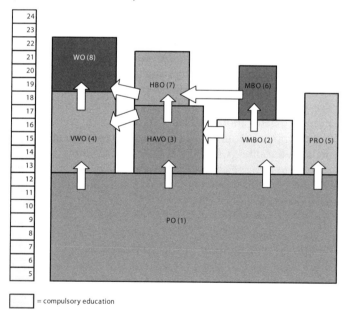

☐ = compulsory education

1 primary education (PO)
2 pre-vocational secondary education (VMBO)
3 senior general secondary education (HAVO)
4 pre-university education (VWO)
5 practical training (PRO)
6 secondary vocational education (MBO): ½-4 yrs
7 higher professional education (HBO-bachelor)
8 university (WO-bachelor + -master)

Source: Ministry of Education (2007: 158)

Most children continue to study after they have gained their secondary school diplomas. The children with a vbo or mavo (or vmbo-t) diploma continue on to middle vocational education (mbo). This could mean a two-, three- or four-year course (either fulltime or part-time). The one- and two-year mbo tracks have an important component of two- to three-day weekly apprenticeships. The one- and two-year mbo tracks will lead to assistant jobs and mostly semi-skilled blue-collar jobs in the labour market. The three- to four-year tracks usually lead to either blue- or white-collar skilled jobs at the middle level.

A unique characteristic of the Dutch school system is that pupils can easily move from one stream to the other. In principle, a pupil could start at the bottom and move up, step by step, to the highest stream (taking the 'long route' through the educational system). Though it may take between one and three years longer for this student than for a non-immigrant pupil to reach the same level, many children of immigrants have moved up the educational ladder in this way.

4.3 Educational priority policies in the Netherlands

The government of the Netherlands was one of the first in Europe to initiate special educational policies for the children of immigrants. In 1985, the Dutch Educational Priority Policy was launched. The cornerstone of this policy was the strong financial injection made available to primary schools with high percentages of pupils from an immigrant background. Primary schools were to receive 1.9 times more funding per pupil of Turkish, Moroccan, Surinamese or Antillean descent (known as CUMI pupils) than for children of parents born in the Netherlands. This provided schools with many children of immigrants a far more generous budget than schools with few or no children of immigrants. Through this mechanism, hundreds of millions of euros have been invested in the primary school education for the children of immigrants over the last 25 years (Crul & Doomernik 2003).

The extra funding in the first years of this policy change was spent mostly on creating smaller classes, but this did not bring the results hoped for (De Jong 1997: 160-163). The idea was that the teacher would be better able to provide individual help and support. Nevertheless, the percentage of immigrant children in these schools continued to rise to the point where more than 70 per cent of children in some schools were from immigrant backgrounds. In practice, this means that ten to fifteen of the twenty pupils in any given class had learning difficulties. Even though the teacher would not have to be responsible for 30 to 35 pupils, as in other primary schools, it was still impossible to give individual attention to each child. Schools increasingly started to focus on new teaching methods, especially those aimed at second-language education. The new teaching methods and books were often financed with extra grants from the city (made available to the larger cities through the national budget). As a result, conditions in schools with many children of immigrants have improved. The classes in these schools are smaller now (ten to fifteen pupils fewer than in a class with 70 per cent or more children of parents born in the Netherlands). Moreover, they often have an extra teaching assistant, the newest teaching methods and books, as well as the best facilities in terms of classrooms and available space.

Secondary schools also get extra funding for CUMI pupils. Another extra source of funding for secondary schools is for so-called Lwoo[4] pupils, students who need extra help and support based on a special test in the last year of primary school. For these pupils, additional individual assistance is available. A large proportion of the Lwoo pupils are from an immigrant background. About a third of pupils of Turkish and Moroccan descent are labelled Lwoo pupils. Secondary schools use most of their CUMI money to reduce the number of pupils in vmbo classes and to employ extra assistance for Dutch-as-a-second-language classes for more recently arrived pupils from abroad. Most of the Lwoo funding is spent on hiring extra teaching or assistant staff.

4.4 Overview of the educational position of pupils and students of Moroccan and Turkish descent

The educational priority policies have resulted in gradually improving results for most children of immigrants in primary schools.[5] National test scores at the end of primary school show that children of immigrants are slowly closing the gap separating them from children of parents born in the Netherlands. This also slowly affects the size of the group that enters the pre-academic streams in secondary education. However, the majority of pupils of Moroccan and Turkish descent in secondary education are still to be found in the lowest streams of secondary school: lower vocational education (vbo) or lower general secondary education (mavo). Both streams are now combined in vmbo. Only about 20 per cent of the pupils of Turkish and Moroccan descent are to be found in the pre-academic tracks that lead directly to higher education (Gijsbert & Herwijer 2007: 11). Dropout rates for the two groups in secondary schools have decreased over the years. The most recent figures show that only 3 per cent of the children of Turkish or Moroccan descent dropped out of secondary school without a diploma (Gijsberts & Herwijer 2007: 115).

The majority (about 75 per cent) of the pupils of Turkish and Moroccan descent enter middle vocational education after secondary school (Gijsbert & Herwijer 2007: 117). Half of them follows the one- to two-year tracks in middle vocational education, and the other half follows the more prestigious three- or four-year tracks (Gijsbert & Herwijer 2007: 118). Dropout rates for the one- and two-year tracks are exceptionally high (for the one-year track, more than 40 per cent drops out). Children who drop out or only have a diploma of one year of middle vocational education in the Netherlands are officially called 'at risk' youth. According to the most recent figures of 2006, 56 per cent of the second-generation Moroccan youth and 63 per cent of second-generation Turkish youth between the ages of twenty and 34 who have already finished school can officially be labelled 'at risk' youth (Turkenburg & Gijsbert 2007: 81).

Those who are on a four-year mbo track (about a third of the pupils of Turkish and Moroccan descent) can potentially continue on to higher education. In 2006 about a third of the nineteen- and twenty-year-old youths of Turkish or Moroccan descent was found in higher education (Jennissen & Hartgens 2006: 20). Since we know that about 20 per cent of the students of Turkish or Moroccan descent takes the direct route to higher education, about 15 per cent has reached higher education through the so-called long route through mbo.[6]

4.5 TIES respondents: entry into school

It is often suggested that early entry into school is beneficial for second-generation pupils. Entering the educational system at a young age means they have the opportunity to acquire the language of the country of residence. Future disadvantages could be avoided by getting accustomed to the educational setting at a young age. In line with this, Dutch policy has put emphasis on the importance of minority children attending crèches and pre-schooling programmes.

The results from the TIES survey show that the second generation of Turkish and Moroccan origin enters some type of school/preschool later than is the case for the comparison group (Table 4.1). We do not find significant differences in entry age between the sexes or between those living in Amsterdam and Rotterdam. The median age for entry into school or, for that matter, preschool is around four years of age among all groups. This seems to imply that the first school experience of most children is primary school rather than a preschool.

Results on crèche attendance confirm these initial findings (Table 4.2). The second generation differs significantly from the comparison group in this respect. Around a third of the Turkish second generation

Table 4.1 *Entry into preschool or school, by age and mean ages*

	Second generation		
Age in years	Turks	Moroccans	Comparison group
2	4.0	1.7	8.3
3	9.8	10.4	22.7
4	75.7	79.2	63.6
5	7.5	5.2	4.3
6	2.9	2.3	0.9
7	0.0	1.2	0
Total	100.0	100.0	100.0
N	499	489	512
Mean	3.95	3.99	3.66

Table 4.2 *Attendance of preschool, by ethnic group and age group*

	18-24	25-29	30-35	Total	N
Second-generation Turks					
No	62.2	71.4	78.6	68.5	333
Yes	37.8	28.6	21.4	31.5	141
Total	100.0	100.0	100.0	100.0	474
Second-generation Moroccans					
No	72.0	80.0	70.6	74.0	334
Yes	28.0	20.0	29.4	26.0	128
Total	100.0	100.0	100.0	100.0	462
Comparison group					
No	28.6	25.1	38.9	32.0	153
Yes	71.4	74.9	61.1	68.0	333
Total	100.0	100.0	100.0	100.0	486

and a quarter of the Moroccan second generation report having attended a crèche. This percentage is substantially higher among the comparison group, two-thirds of which have attended a crèche. It is interesting to note, however, that among the Turkish second generation and the comparison group, the younger cohorts were particularly more likely to have attended crèches than the older ones. Boys are overall somewhat more likely to have been in preschool than girls.

4.6 Primary education

For many children, entering primary education is the start of an educational career. Recent debates have pointed more and more to differences in the quality and subsequent results achieved by schools in primary education. But what guides the choice for choosing a specific primary school? And do these reasons differ between groups?

Our analyses show that the most important reason for attending a specific primary school was its location in the neighbourhood where the family lives (Table 4.3). Although this reason was by far the most important among all groups, it was even more predominant among the second generation than it is for the comparison group. The answers given by Turkish and Moroccan young adults do not differ significantly on this point. The second reason most often mentioned was that the decision for choosing a school was left to the parents. For young adults of the comparison group, this reason was more important than for the second generation. For the Turkish and Moroccan second generation, the third major reason was having siblings already at the school. Although young adults from the comparison group mention this reason just as often, their third most important deciding factor was the school's religious denomination. The school's reputation was only important for around 10 per cent of all groups.

Practical considerations, like proximity and siblings at school, thus seem to guide the choice of a primary school more than arguments about school quality and educational philosophy do. This is particularly the case for second-generation Turkish and Moroccan young adults. For the Moroccan second generation we find, however, that the youngest group (between eighteen and 24 years old) more often mentions school quality as being an important factor in their choice than do older Moroccan respondents. For the Turkish second generation and the comparison group, a stable percentage over the age groups (around 10 per cent) reports this factor to be of relevance. Analysis of differences between the age groups also reveals that the youngest Turkish and

Table 4.3 *Reasons given for choosing a primary school in %, by ethnic group*

	Second generation		Comparison group
	Turks	Moroccans	
School in neighbourhood	79.3	80.5	52.1
School without religious denomination	3.4	2.3	9.9
Good reputation	8.0	10.3	9.8
Educational philosophy	0.6	0.6	7.1
Religious denomination	2.3	2.3	16.2
Parents decided	21.3	20.1	37.7
Siblings already attended school	14.4	16.7	13.3
Few immigrants	1.7	1.1	0.6
Acceptance policy school	0.6	0.0	0.3
Other	4.6	2.9	4.5
N	500	493	512

Note: Percentages do not add up to 100 because respondents could give more than one reason.

Moroccan respondents (eighteen to 24 years) mentioned that their parents decided more often than was the case for the older respondents. The reverse was true for the comparison group: the younger cohorts reported less often that the parents decided. Our findings, furthermore, indicate that the choice for a certain school seems to be rather stable: only around a third of all respondents ever changed their primary schools. No significant differences were found between each of the groups included in the study.

School is one of the potential places children of both immigrant and native Dutch origins can meet. There is great debate about segregation in the educational system and its effects on school results, processes of integration and the society at large. The TIES survey provides insight into how school classes in primary education were composed with regard to ethnic origin. Table 4.4 gives an overview of the share of immigrant children at primary school distinguished by age group. Overall, it is obvious that most young second-generation Turks and Moroccans attended primary schools where a substantial share of the children was of immigrant origin. Respondents of the comparison group had more limited encounters with children of immigrants. At the same time, there are clear differences between each of the age groups. The percentage of respondents claiming that they had no children of immigrants at their primary schools declines per age group as well as for all groups. This clearly reflects the changes in the ethnic composition of Dutch society. However, ethnic segregation also seems to have increased: around half of the youngest group of the second generation attended a primary

Table 4.4 *Share of children of immigrants at primary school, by ethnic group and age group*

	Age	Almost none	1/4	1/2	3/4	Almost all	Total	Mean (1-5= none-all)	N
Second-generation Turks	18-24	7.0	12.8	30.2	26.7	23.3	100.0		253
	25-29	6.9	25.9	20.7	24.1	22.4	100.0		159
	30-36	25.9	33.3	29.6	7.4	3.7	100.0		75
	Total	10.0	21.0	27.0	23.0	20.0	100.0	3.2	487
Second-generation Moroccans	18-24	5.3	19.5	29.2	26.5	19.5	100.0		314
	25-29	9.8	31.7	39.0	9.8	9.8	100.0		119
	30-36	31.3	25.0	31.3	0.0	12.5	100.0		52
	Total	9.0	23.0	32.0	20.0	16.0	100.0	3.1	485
Comparison group	18-24	57.3	23.6	13.1	5.1	1.0	100.0		151
	25-29	71.2	18.9	8.1	1.7	0.0	100.0		156
	30-36	79.7	16.2	2.5	1.6	0.0	100.0		201
	Total	71.0	19.0	7.0	3.0	0.0	100.0	1.4	508

Table 4.5 *Ever repeated classes, by ethnic group and sex*

	Second generation				Comparison group	
	Turks		Moroccans			
	Men	Women	Men	Women	Men	Women
Yes	23.8	22.2	24.4	20.0	12.3	7.4
No	76.2	77.8	75.6	80.0	87.7	92.6
Total	100.0	100.0	100.0	100.0	100.0	100.0
N	242	258	246	247	250	262

school where three-quarters of the students were of immigrant origin. On the contrary, almost 60 per cent of the youngest comparison group youth in the TIES survey had no (or almost no) children of immigrants in their school; another 24 per cent had a quarter at most.

A larger share of the second generation than the comparison group respondents has repeated classes in primary education (Table 4.5). Men among all groups are slightly more likely to have repeated classes, though the differences between men and women are not significant.

The literature has suggested that substantial shares of children of immigrants spend some time abroad, most often in their parents' country of origin. Our data suggest that only a small percentage (7 per cent) of the Turkish and Moroccan second generation, overall, spend more than three months abroad during their period of primary education (Table 4.6). We observe clear differences between the younger and older age groups of the second generation, however. Almost 30 per cent of the Moroccan second generation currently between 30 and 36 years of age report having spent more than three months abroad. By contrast, only 2 per cent of Moroccans aged eighteen to 24 years has been abroad for a longer period. A similar pattern applies to the Turkish second generation in the TIES survey.

A crucial stage of school career in the Netherlands is the school recommendation students receive at the end of primary education. This is the moment when students are tracked into different educational le-

Table 4.6 *Percentage ever spent more than three months abroad during primary education, by age group and ethnic group*

	Second generation		
Age	Turks	Moroccans	Comparison group
18-24	3.4	1.8	1.6
25-29	8.5	11.9	2.3
30-36	18.5	29.4	2.7
Total	8.0	8.0	2.0
N	500	493	512

Table 4.7 *School advice at the end of primary education, by ethnic group*

	Second generation		Comparison group
	Turks	Moroccans	
Lower vocational education (vbo or vmbo basis or vmbo kader)	24.3	26.2	13.5
Mixed advice: Lower vocational education and lower general secondary education (vbo/mavo)	16.1	11.6	4.2
Lower general secondary education (mavo or vmbo-theoretisch)	21.8	21.3	7.9
Mixed advice: Lower general secondary education or higher general secondary education (mavo/havo)	18.6	15.2	14.0
Higher general secondary education (havo)	7.5	9.8	14.0
Mixed advice: Higher general secondary education and preparatory tertiary education (havo/vwo)	6.8	10.4	25.5
Preparatory tertiary education or gymnasium (vwo or gymnasium)	5.0	5.5	21.1
Total	100.0	100.0	100.0
N	458	465	491

vels. Table 4.7 gives a detailed overview of the school recommendations that second-generation Turks and Moroccans and the comparison group received by the end of their primary education.

The majority (about 60 per cent) of Turkish and Moroccan second-generation youth get a recommendation for, at best, lower general secondary education level. By contrast, we find that 60 per cent of the comparison group was recommended for higher general secondary education or better. Only 19 and 25 per cent of second-generation Turks and Moroccans, respectively, get this recommendation. The four most common school recommendations received by both Turkish and Moroccan young adults are for the lowest level, the middle level, a mixed level or an in-between level. This indicates that such pupils can access the middle level, though if they work hard, they could also complete a higher level. It is apparent that overall recommendations for the second generation are significantly lower than for the comparison group. We find no differences in recommendation between the sexes for any of the groups.

4.7 Secondary education

After students receive a recommendation from their primary school, they begin the selection process of where to pursue secondary education. Parents and children are free to choose the school, and secondary schools compete for new students. Again, we find that the most important reason guiding the choice of a school for secondary education is its proximity to home (Table 4.8). The second most common reason is the reputation of a particular school, something a quarter of all respondents among all groups mentioned. However, for the second generation, we found that siblings' attendance at the school and the primary school recommendation were the decisive factors in their choice. Although proximity to home was also mentioned by the comparison group, the primary school recommendation was less often cited as a reason for their secondary school choice. Twenty per cent of the young adults of the comparison group state that their parents decided on the particular school; the second generation mentions this reason significantly less often.

The composition of the secondary schools attended by the second-generation and comparison group youth clearly differs, as is shown in Table 4.9. The majority of the second generation attended schools where at least half of the school population was of immigrant origin. By far, the greater part of young adults of the comparison group were at secondary schools where no or, at most, a quarter of the students had an immigrant background. Over time, there seems to be an increase in the concentration of the second generation in schools where more students are of immigrant background. This is particularly clear for the Moroccan second generation. Although the secondary schools of the comparison group's younger cohorts among young adults seem to be more ethnically mixed, they continue to attend schools with small percentages of children of immigrants.

We further analysed whether there were differences in the reported ethnic background of the student population between those growing up in

Table 4.8 *Reasons given for choosing a secondary school in %, by ethnic group*

	Second generation		Comparison group
	Turks	Moroccans	
School in neighbourhood	32.8	29.3	24.0
School without religious denomination	2.9	1.1	5.7
Good reputation	24.7	25.7	23.9
Educational philosophy	0.6	2.3	5.4
Religious denomination	1.1	0.6	6.1
Parents decided	10.3	5.2	19.9
Siblings already attended school	14.4	19.4	16.3
Friends from primary education went there	8.0	8.0	13.3
Few immigrants	1.7	1.1	0.8
Acceptance policy school	0.0	0.0	0.0
Because of school advice	16.1	19.4	11.4
N	500	492	512

Note: Percentages do not add up to 100 because respondents could give more than one reason.

Table 4.9 *Share of children of immigrants at secondary school, by ethnic group and age group*

	Age	Almost none	1/4	1/2	3/4	Almost all	Total	Mean (1-5= none-all)	N
Second-generation Turks	18-24	6.8	13.6	35.2	27.3	17.0	100.0		253
	25-29	5.4	17.9	35.7	25.0	16.1	100.0		156
	30-36	17.9	25.0	32.1	14.3	10.7	100.0		73
	Total	8.0	17.0	35.0	25.0	15.0	100.0	3.2	482
Second-generation Moroccans	18-24	2.6	14.9	35.1	34.2	13.2	100.0		317
	25-29	9.8	14.6	41.5	26.8	7.3	100.0		117
	30-36	18.8	31.3	43.8	6.3	0.0	100.0		50
	Total	6.0	16.0	38.0	30.0	10.0	100.0	3.2	484
Comparison group	18-24	40.9	28.9	17.9	7.5	4.7	100.0		153
	25-29	47.4	36.4	14.2	1.7	0.3	100.0		156
	30-36	58.3	30.2	7.8	2.5	1.2	100.0		201
	Total	50.0	32.0	12.0	3.0	2.0	100.0	1.8	510

the cities or elsewhere in the country (not in table). Young adults of the comparison group who were not living in Amsterdam and Rotterdam between the ages of twelve and sixteen were significantly less likely to encounter children of immigrants in secondary education than those living in the two main cities. For the second generation, we do not find differences among those living in Amsterdam, Rotterdam or anywhere else.

Changing secondary schools is not very common according to the results of the TIES survey (Table 4.10). We find that between 20 and 30 per cent of all students has ever changed their schools. Whereas the percentages of change are pretty similar for the three groups in Amsterdam, we find pronounced differences between the groups for those currently living in Rotterdam. Second-generation Moroccan young adults in Rotterdam changed schools slightly more often than respondents of the comparison group, though these differences are not statistically significant. Second-generation Turkish young adults in Rotterdam, however, were more likely to have changed their secondary school than is the case for the second-generation Moroccans and the comparison

Table 4.10 *Ever changed secondary schools, by city of residence and ethnic group*

	Second generation		Comparison group
	Turks	Moroccans	
Amsterdam	23.9	23.1	23.0
Rotterdam	31.7	29.3	17.5
Total	29.0	25.0	21.0
N	500	492	512

Table 4.11 *Ever repeated classes, by ethnic group*

| | Second generation | | Comparison group |
	Turks	Moroccans	
Yes	36.8	24.0	31.9
No	63.2	76.0	68.1
Total	100.0	100.0	100
N	500	495	512

group. Stays abroad are much less common among all groups (not in table). Just 2 per cent of the Moroccan second generation and 4 per cent of the Turkish second generation reported staying abroad for more than three months during their secondary education.

Having to repeat classes in secondary school is much more common among all groups (Table 4.11) than it is in primary school. In total, 24 per cent of all second-generation Moroccans, 37 per cent of the second-generation Turks and 32 of the comparison group say they repeated classes in secondary education. Second-generation Moroccans, both men and women, are significantly less likely to have repeated classes than is the case for the other two groups. Among the Turkish second generation and the comparison group, men are more likely to have repeated classes in secondary education than women. For second-generation Moroccans slightly more women than men have repeated classes, though these differences are not significant.

Our survey includes substantial numbers of respondents who are still in some sort of education. A third of the second-generation Turks and comparison group and half of the second-generation Moroccans are still receiving education (not in table). These figures reflect the fact that the Moroccan respondents in the survey are younger than those in the Turkish group and comparison group, and therefore are more likely to be in school. Taking age effects into account, we find that second-generation Turks are more likely to have left the educational system than is the case for the other two groups. Our analysis of achieved educational level (defined by having ascertained a diploma or certificate) pertains only to those who are currently not in education. Table 4.12a provides a detailed overview of realised educational level per group for those no longer in education. The most common level for the Turkish second generation is middle vocational education (mbo). The same applies for the Moroccan second generation. Around 85 per cent of the young adults in both groups have a diploma at the mbo level, at best. In contrast, we see that three-quarters of the young adults of the comparison group has at least an mbo diploma. For the Turkish and Moroccan second generation, we find that about 10 per cent finished primary education. This indicates that they dropped out in secondary education without acquiring a diplo-

Table 4.12a *Highest educational level for those currently not in education, by ethnic group and sex*

	Second generation				Comparison group	
	Turks		Moroccans			
	Men	Women	Men	Women	Men	Women
Primary school (basisschool/lagere school)	8.5	8.6	10.0	10.3	0.8	0.8
Individual or special education (proo[a] or ivbo[b] or speciaal onderwijs)	2.1	3.4	5.0	0.0	0.5	0.3
Lower secondary vocational education (vbo or lhno or lts or vmbo-basis or vmbo-kader)	19.1	10.3	12.5	12.8	9.3	6.7
Lower secondary general education (vmbo-gemengd or mavo or vmbo-theoretisch)	19.1	10.3	20.0	10.3	4.0	4.7
Higher secondary general education (havo)	4.3	5.2	2.5	2.6	3.4	5.2
Preparatory tertiary education (vwo or gymnasium)	0.0	1.7	0.0	2.6	2.9	0.8
Short middle vocational education (kmbo or mbo-niveau 1 or mbo-niveau 2)	14.9	10.3	12.5	15.4	5.0	5.4
Middle vocational education (mbo-niveau 3 or mbo-niveau 4 or mbo)	14.9	37.9	27.5	23.1	16.7	13.2
Higher vocational education (hbo; propedeuse or hbo)	10.6	10.3	10.0	20.5	32.4	31.3
University (universiteit; kandidaats/bachelor or universiteit; doctorandus/Master/PhD)	6.4	1.7	0.0	2.6	24.9	31.8
Total	100.0	100.0	100.0	100.0	100.0	100.0
N	132	158	113	119	167	166

[a] Praktijkonderwijs
[b] Individueel Voorbereidend Beroeps Onderwijs

ma. Broadening the scope to young adults considered at risk – because they were not able to get a diploma even at the mbo-1 level – we find that half of the second generation and a quarter of the comparison group belong to this at-risk group. The other half of the second generation was most likely to finish their education at the mbo level. Around 10 and 14 per cent of second-generation Turks and Moroccans, respectively, have a higher vocational education (hbo) diploma.

We also analysed the current educational level of those young adults who are still in the educational system (Table 4.12b). We find that a majority of all respondents is currently attending school at a minimum of an mbo-4 level. Around a third of the second-generation youth who are in education is at the hbo, while smaller percentages are found at the

EDUCATION   77

Table 4.12b *Current educational level for those who are in education, by ethnic group and sex*

	Second generation				Comparison group	
	Turks		Moroccans			
	Men	Women	Men	Women	Men	Women
Individual or special education (proo[a] or ivbo[b] or speciaal onderwijs)	0.0	0.0	0.0	0.0	0.0	0.0
Lower secondary vocational education (vbo or lhno or lts or vmbo-basis or vmbo-kader)	6.3	3.6	6.5	2.3	1.9	1.0
Lower secondary general education (vmbo-gemengd or mavo or vmbo-theoretisch)	6.3	7.1	4.3	9.1	0.0	0.0
Higher secondary general education (havo)	0.0	0.0	4.3	2.3	0.0	1.5
Preparatory tertiary education (vwo or gymnasium)	0.0	0.0	2.2	4.5	7.1	8.6
Short middle vocational education (kmbo or mbo-niveau 1 or mbo-niveau 2)	15.6	14.3	13.0	9.1	1.9	2.5
Middle vocational education (mbo-niveau 3 or mbo-niveau 4 or mbo)	25.0	28.6	30.4	29.5	9.6	10.6
Higher vocational education (hbo; propedeuse or hbo)	28.1	42.9	26.1	34.1	28.8	35.9
University (universiteit; kandidaats/bachelor or universiteit; doctorandus/Master/PhD)	18.8	3.6	13.0	9.1	50.6	39.9
Total	100.0	100.0	100.0	100.0	100.0	100.0
N	100	92	126	123	77	89

[a] Praktijkonderwijs
[b] Individueel Voorbereidend Beroeps Onderwijs

university level. Although a similar share of young adults of the comparison group is found at the hbo level, they are significantly more often found to be pursuing the academic track.

4.8 Experiences at school

The school can shape the climate in which children are stimulated to learn and develop themselves. Respondents in the survey were asked to look back on their secondary education and report on their experiences. First of all, we studied the percentage of students who received special attention in school, through remedial teaching, or outside school, in the form of homework tutoring (Table 4.13). Only a minority of the young adults have had remedial teaching. We do not find differences between the groups on this point. A much larger proportion of the young adults has had homework tutoring at some point: 18 per cent of the second-

Table 4.13 *Ever had remedial teaching or homework counselling at secondary school in %, by ethnic group*

	Second generation		Comparison group
	Turks	Moroccans	
Remedial teaching	6.0	8.0	8.0
Homework counselling	17.8	23.6	18.9
N	500	492	512

generation Turks and 24 per cent of the second-generation Moroccans say they have had homework tutoring. These percentages are similar for the comparison group. Unfortunately, we do not have information on how often or for how long use was made of homework tutoring, nor do we know how the students found their way to these homework tutoring groups.

Table 4.14 provides an overview of how much respondents agreed with three statements on their relationships with teachers in secondary education. Overall, the young adults report that they could get along well with their teachers; between 81 and 86 per cent of the respondents agree or totally agree with this statement. The three groups do not differ among one other on this point. Women are generally somewhat more positive about their relationship with teachers than men are; women more often agree totally with the statement that they could get along well with their teachers (not in table). This difference is most pronounced for the second generation and for students of Turkish descent, in particular. In line with the overall positive evaluation of their relationship with teachers is the finding that 60 per cent of all respondents report that their teachers really listened to what they had to say. Another quarter neither agreed nor disagreed with this statement. We do not find significant differences between the groups. Women, particularly those of Turkish origin, are more likely to feel that teachers really 'heard' what they had to say (not in table). Finally, the young adults were asked whether they received help from teachers when needed. As many as seven out of every ten young adults state that they did receive extra help when needed. The Moroccan second generation is somewhat more positive about the help they received from teachers than is the comparison group. In line with the positive evaluation of their relationship with teachers overall, we find that women more often than men report that teachers gave them help when needed (not in table). Although this pattern is apparent for all groups, it is most pronounced among the second generation.

Finally, our results show that a relatively small share of Turkish (15 per cent) and Moroccan (6 per cent) second-generation respondents felt less

Table 4.14 *Description of relationships with teachers, by ethnic group*

		Second generation		Comparison group
		Turks	Moroccans	
Could get along well with teachers	Totally agree	37.4	32.8	28.3
	Agree	43.7	52.9	54.7
	Neutral	10.9	9.2	8.4
	Do not agree	5.2	3.4	7.8
	Totally disagree	2.9	1.7	0.8
	Total	100.0	100.0	100.0
	N	500	492	512
Most teachers really listened	Totally agree	19.5	14.9	9.4
	Agree	42.0	50.3	52.5
	Neutral	25.3	21.7	24.6
	Do not agree	9.8	10.3	9.9
	Totally disagree	3.4	2.9	3.6
	Total	100.0	100.0	100.0
	N	500	492	512
Teachers provided extra help when needed	Totally agree	20.7	23.6	16.3
	Agree	55.2	57.5	55.5
	Neutral	14.9	12.1	18.8
	Do not agree	6.9	5.7	8.1
	Totally disagree	2.3	1.1	1.3
	Total	100.0	100.0	100.0
	N	500	492	512

welcome at school than their Dutch peers. The large majority of the second generation report feeling at least as welcome at secondary education as students of the comparison group (not in table): 75 per cent of the second-generation Turkish and 87 per cent of the second-generation Moroccan young adults. When asked about how often Turks or Moroccans experience hostility or unfairness at school based on their origin, we found that 40 per cent of all respondents think this occurs sometimes. One-fifth reported thinking such experiences are rare, while another fifth thinks origin-based acts of bias happen regularly. We do not find significant differences between the second generation and comparison group on this point. In addition, reports by second-generation men and women are not significantly different. For the comparison group, we find that more women than men are of the opinion that Turks and Moroccans experience more hostility at school. It is interesting to note that Moroccans in Amsterdam feel that hostility at school takes place more often than is the case for the Moroccans in Rotterdam (11 versus 6 per cent). For the Turkish second generation, we find the opposite: those living in Rotterdam are more of the opinion that Turks and Moroccans are experiencing hostility in school than those in Amsterdam (14 versus 7 per cent).

4.9 The parental home and education

Besides the experiences at school, it is important to know more about the situation in the parental home. Parents and siblings may have an important role in shaping the educational experiences of youth of different origins. Asked about the possibility of having a quiet space in the home to do homework, a large majority of respondents among all groups indicated that they had such a place (not in table). Nevertheless, we find that second-generation Turkish and Moroccans young adults were less likely to have such a place than the comparison group (85 versus 95 per cent). The comparison group had many more books available at the parental home. About half of all respondents of the comparison group had more than 100 books at home, whereas a third of all Turks and Moroccans had access to no more than ten books at home.

The respondents in the survey were asked to report how important certain persons were for their education and schooling while they were in secondary education. Table 4.15 gives an overview, by ethnic group, of the importance attached to parents, teachers, peers and siblings. Among all groups, around three-quarters of the young adults felt their mothers were very important or important. Mothers seem to be most important for the schooling of children. However, our results also point to paternal importance: around two-thirds of the second-generation Turkish and comparison group young adults and three-quarters of the second-generation Moroccans felt their fathers were important. Although fathers are important for two-thirds of respondents in all groups, this does not significantly differ from the importance attached to teachers across each of the groups. It is nevertheless clear that the second generation evaluates teachers' importance more highly than the comparison group does. For peers and siblings, we find interesting differences between the second-generation groups and the comparison group. For the second generation, particularly among Moroccans, older siblings are more important than peers, whereas the reverse is true for the comparison group. One should certainly bear in mind here that young adults of the comparison group are much less likely to have older siblings than is the case for the second generation. When taking the number of older siblings into account in the analyses, the expressed group differences remain (not in table). Overall, we find that women more often feel that family members and others were very important for their schooling than men.

Table 4.15 *Description of others' impact on education while in secondary school, by ethnic group and sex*

	Second generation				Comparison group	
	Turks		Moroccans			
	Men	Women	Men	Women	Men	Women
Mother						
Not important at all	7.2	4.5	3.4	2.4	2.4	2.5
Not important	8.4	5.7	6.9	7.2	12.1	3.5
Little important	14.5	14.8	10.3	9.6	18.8	12.8
Important	32.5	26.1	36.8	28.9	39.0	35.8
Very important	37.3	48.9	42.5	51.8	27.8	45.3
Total	100.0	100.0	100.0	100.0	100.0	100.0
N	240	250	238	245	249	257
Father						
Not important at all	7.6	7.0	3.5	4.9	5.7	6.9
Not important	15.2	11.6	7.1	6.2	14.9	6.9
Little important	19.0	12.8	12.9	9.9	26.5	13.8
Important	29.1	29.1	29.4	28.4	37.2	40.9
Very important	29.1	39.5	47.1	50.6	15.6	31.5
Total	100.0	100.0	100.0	100.0	100.0	100.0
N	229	243	233	230	240	253
Teacher						
Not important at all	3.7	0.0	2.3	2.4	4.4	3.4
Not important	11.0	9.1	8.0	7.1	13.3	6.6
Little important	28.0	17.0	14.8	17.6	25.6	32.0
Important	39.0	50.0	53.4	45.9	47.2	46.8
Very important	18.0	23.9	21.6	27.1	9.5	11.2
Total	100.0	100.0	100.0	100.0	100.0	100.0
N	238	252	243	246	250	261
Peers						
Not important at all	9.5	3.4	5.7	3.6	5.4	4.6
Not important	19.0	14.8	20.5	16.7	20.5	8.5
Little important	33.3	30.7	39.8	28.6	32.9	24.1
Important	29.8	39.8	28.4	38.1	34.2	43.0
Very important	8.3	11.4	5.7	13.1	7.0	19.8
Total	100.0	100.0	100.0	100.0	100.0	100.0
N	239	251	242	245	248	262
Older siblings						
Not important at all	7.1	9.3	3.0	1.6	8.1	6.3
Not important	12.5	7.4	10.4	12.5	33.9	22.7
Little important	25.0	24.1	20.9	15.6	30.2	23.6
Important	30.4	33.3	41.8	37.5	20.0	36.0
Very important	25.0	25.9	23.9	32.8	7.8	11.5
Total	100.0	100.0	100.0	100.0	100.0	100.0
N	158	154	182	188	136	143

Comparison of the relative importance of each of the parents (not in table) shows that, among all groups, the importance attached to fathers and mothers is equal: ranging from 58 per cent for the comparison group to 73 per cent among the Moroccan second generation. However, the percentage of young adults for whom the role of the mother was larger than that of the father is highest for the comparison group. Among them, a third evaluates their mother as more important than their father. Mothers are, in general, also found to be more important than peers and teachers. At the same time, around a third of all respondents in all three groups evaluates their mothers and teachers as being equally important.

Parents can be involved in school and education in very different ways. The young adults in the survey were asked about practical aspects of parental involvement in their education (Table 4.16). Parents of the second generation, particularly those of Moroccan origin, checked how much time their children spent on homework significantly more often than those in the comparison group. However, according to our respondents, comparison group parents helped significantly more with homework than did Moroccan and Turkish parents. Education and schooling were most often discussed in Turkish families, then followed by comparison group families and, finally, Moroccan families. Although Moroccan parents reportedly did not speak with their children about education, as was the case for the other groups, Moroccan parents were more often in touch with teachers than was the case for the other two groups.

The way in which parents are involved in their children's education is highly comparable overall. We find that Turkish and Moroccan parents seem to be in touch with their daughters' teachers somewhat more often than is the case for their sons, and girls of the comparison group seem to get somewhat more help with their homework than do boys. The most striking gender differences are not directly related to school, but are found in the involvement in household chores. In particular, in Turkish families, boys are less likely to have to do household chores than girls are.

In line with the importance attached to older brothers and sisters, we find that siblings helped with homework most often among the second-generation Moroccans followed by the Turkish and comparison group (not in table). Similar patterns were found when talking about education or school. Older siblings seem thus to be much more important for the education of their younger siblings in Moroccan families than they are in Turkish families and comparison group families.

Table 4.16 Involvement of parents in schooling, by ethnic group and sex

	Second generation				Comparison group	
	Turks		Moroccans			
	Men	Women	Men	Women	Men	Women
Parents checked how much time was spent on homework						
Very often	13.3	12.4	15.9	22.4	5.3	6.6
Often	22.9	24.7	34.1	30.6	25.5	19.2
Sometimes	26.5	27.0	26.1	22.4	31.1	22.3
Not often	18.1	20.2	13.6	11.8	21.2	30.2
Never	19.3	15.7	10.2	12.9	16.8	21.7
Total	100.0	100.0	100.0	100.0	100.0	100.0
N	240	253	243	246	250	261
Parents helped with homework						
Very often	2.4	2.3	4.6	7.0	2.2	7.2
Often	8.4	10.2	10.3	11.6	11.9	22.3
Sometimes	21.7	17.0	25.3	25.6	36.6	42.3
Not often	18.1	19.3	20.7	19.8	34.0	19.0
Never	49.4	51.1	39.1	36.0	15.2	9.2
Total	100.0	100.0	100.0	100.0	100.0	100.0
N	240	253	242	246	249	261
Parents talked about school and learning						
Very often	11.9	17.2	20.5	26.2	4.8	15.5
Often	35.7	42.5	46.6	44.0	54.2	52.1
Sometimes	33.3	27.6	22.7	21.4	29.1	25.2
Not often	13.1	5.7	8.0	6.0	9.1	5.1
Never	6.0	6.9	2.3	2.4	2.8	2.1
Total	100.0	100.0	100.0	100.0	100.0	100.0
N	240	251	242	246	249	261
Parents were in touch with teachers						
Very often	6.0	12.6	8.2	13.1	4.3	6.3
Often	23.8	32.2	32.9	33.3	24.5	21.5
Sometimes	44.0	34.5	41.2	35.7	43.3	43.7
Not often	16.7	11.5	14.1	13.1	24.3	24.8
Never	9.5	9.2	3.5	4.8	3.5	3.8
Total	100.0	100.0	100.0	100.0	100.0	100.0
N	240	250	241	246	249	260
Respondent performed household chores/babysitting						
Very often	1.2	3.4	2.3	7.1	4.6	2.5
Often	7.1	15.9	12.6	16.5	24.9	17.6
Sometimes	23.8	28.4	36.8	36.5	41.4	49.1
Not often	26.2	23.9	23.0	22.4	18.8	18.8
Never	41.7	28.4	25.3	17.6	10.2	12.0
Total	100.0	100.0	100.0	100.0	100.0	100.0
N	240	252	242	246	249	261

4.10 Conclusions

Based on the overview of different indicators of school performance presented in this chapter, we can draw some initial albeit cautious conclusions on the position of the second generation in education. The TIES survey results can be interpreted in different ways. It is the classic half-full-or-half-empty glass dilemma. When we look at the group of second-generation young adults who have already left school, the results are rather alarming: about half could officially be labelled as at-risk youth. This percentage is twice as high as what we find among the comparison group. This very negative picture, however, changes when we take those who are still in education into account: this group of the second generation performs remarkably well. More than 40 per cent of them is in higher education. Both trends seem to operate simultaneously: we find that a considerable group stays behind and an equally large group performs remarkably well. The fact that such a substantial share of the second generation seems to do pretty well in school is even more outstanding when one considers how little schooling their parents have generally had.

Another important observation from these first analyses relates to changes over time. If we distinguish between different age cohorts of the current second generation, we find remarkable developments. To name the most important ones: over time, more second-generation youth attend preschools, they are more often found in a segregated school situation (both in primary and secondary schools) and they interrupt primary school less often for a stay in Turkey or Morocco. A final interesting finding is that the majority of second-generation youth, like the comparison group, is very positive about the role of teachers in school. In general, second-generation youth also stress the important roles parents and siblings play in their success at school. Family members being important actors in their lives, however, is more emphasised among the second generation than the comparison group.

Notes

1 Voorbereidend Beroeps Onderwijs.
2 Middelbaar Algemeen Voortgezet Onderwijs; Voorbereidend Middelbaar Beroepsonderwijs-theoretisch.
3 Hoger Algemeen Voortgezet Onderwijs; Voorbereidend Wetenschappelijk Onderwijs.
4 Leerwegondersteunend onderwijs.
5 We do need to take into consideration that some of the improvement stems from more second-generation children entering the educational system from the beginning.
6 Middelbaar Beroeps Onderwijs.

References

Crul, M. & J. Doomernik (2003), 'The Turkish and the Moroccan Second Generation in the Netherlands: Divergent Trends between and Polarization within the Two Groups', *International Migration Review* 37(4): 1039-1065.

De Jong, M. (1997), 'De taak van het onderwijs en de volwasseneducatie binnen een actief inburgerschapsbeleid', in M. Foblets & B. Hubeay (eds.), *Nieuwe burgers in de Samenleving?*, 155-171. Leuven: Acco.

Gijsberts M. & L. Herweijer (2007), 'Allochtone leerlingen in het Onderwijs', in J. Dagevos & M. Gijsberts (eds.), *Jaarrapport Integratie 2007*, 102-130. The Hague: SCP.

Jennissen R. & M. Hartgens (2006), 'Allochtonen in het onderwijs', in *Integratiekaart 2006*, 11-24. The Hague: WOCD.

Ministry of Education (2007), *EURYDICE: The educational system in the Netherlands 2007*. The Hague: Ministry of Education.

Turkenburg, M. & M. Gijsberts (2007), 'Opleidingsniveau en beheersing van de Nederlandse taal', in J. Dagevos & M. Gijsberts (eds.), *Jaarrapport Integratie 2007*, 72-101. The Hague: SCP.

5 Labour and income

Liesbeth Heering and Susan ter Bekke

5.1 Introduction

This chapter describes the labour market and income situation of the three groups studied. We will present an overview of the current situation of the TIES respondents with respect to work. In section 5.4, we will also look at the transition from school or study to work, as well as job and unemployment levels. As section 5.5 shows, through work, scholarships, unemployment or other social benefits an income is acquired, and we will thus examine both the main source of respondents' income and the amounts they earn. In section 5.6, we will report how respondents describe feelings of personal and group discrimination in the labour market. The aim here is to explore conditions for success or failure in the Dutch labour market by analysing the extent to which people of different ethnic backgrounds participate and have equal work access. We will pay particular attention to differences between men and women in labour behaviour, choices and experiences. Section 5.2 gives a brief overview of Dutch labour market policies addressing ethnic minorities and sketches the development of their situation in the labour market in the past ten years. Because the two ethnic groups in our study are part of a greater population of non-western ethnic minorities – and information is only available for them as a whole – we will sometimes refer to this larger group of minorities. Section 5.3 portrays the current situation in Amsterdam and Rotterdam.

5.2 Ethnic minorities in labour market policies

In the annual Integration Report 2007, Dagevos and Gijsberts remark that, 'The proportion of members of non-western ethnic minorities in employment is substantially higher today than it was ten years ago, while unemployment is substantially lower' (Dagevos & Gijsberts 2007: 317). The level of unemployment among the population of non-western descent is still high at 16 per cent, as compared with 4 per cent for the population of Dutch descent. The gap in unemployment level between the two populations has narrowed by 7 percentage points in this period.

The high unemployment of the ethnic minorities in the labour force is mainly a problem of high youth unemployment. More than one in five (22 per cent) of the ethnic minorities population between fifteen and 24 years of age are without work versus 9 per cent of their Dutch counterparts. However, this relatively high figure is a big improvement over the situation of ten years earlier, when 35 per cent of the young ethnic minorities was unemployed. The developments in the two ethnic groups of our study are in line with the general trends. Ten years ago, around one-third of Turks and Moroccans aged between fifteen and 65 had paid work for at least twelve hours a week, while, in 2006, around 45 per cent had paid work. While the improvements have been progressive and are thus encouraging, there is still a great gap in net participation between the second-generation population and that of Dutch descent – of which 67 per cent has paid work.

Long ago, the government began general labour market initiatives to tackle youth unemployment by creating subsidised jobs for the bottom end of the labour market. Ethnic minorities have always been explicitly mentioned as a vulnerable group needing extra help due to high unemployment. Most of the policies that benefit the second generation are general policies. Since the second generation entered the labour market at the beginning of the 1990s, we will only discuss the relevant policies from that time onwards. With the publication of *Contourennota* (Contours Report) in 1994, the socio-economic aspects of integration were given more prominence, as evidenced by integration policies. Moreover, the first Purple Coalition government (1994-1998) created measures and launched projects to target young people from those ethnic minority groups with difficulties transitioning to the labour market (Smeets et al. 1999: 33). The measures of this period aimed to remove barriers for people with an immigrant background as well as to promote general facilities and programmes, such as subsidised job schemes. Municipalities were responsible for the implementation and coordination. After four years in existence, by 1998, 40,000 people had participated in the biggest job scheme ever implemented, the Wet Inschakeling Werkzoekenden (Act Involving Jobseekers). Two-thirds of the beneficiaries of the scheme were people of Dutch descent and about a quarter had a non-western background. In the latter group, 5 per cent was of Turkish and 5 per cent of Moroccan descent. These programmes primarily reached people of the first generation (Martens & Weijers 2000: 60).

To fight discrimination and to encourage companies to employ people of immigrant descent, several measures were taken. The Wet Samen (Act Stimulating Labour Participation of Minorities 1998-2004) as well as its prior rendition, the Wbeaa 1994-1998 (Act Encouraging Equal Labour Participation), are viewed by the government as two of the programme's most important instruments (Dagevos 2001: 90).

From 1998 onwards, companies with more than 35 employees were obliged to register their personnel according to their descent. Annual reports had to include a plan of action that would improve the inflow of personnel of foreign descent and encourage their promotion to better jobs. Although companies initially resisted the law and were disinclined to cooperate with reporting, the situation improved over the course of time. An evaluation of the law in 2000 concluded that the Wet Samen's main achievement was its capacity to improve awareness of the issues at stake. In general, personnel policies did not change very much, and only rarely were quantitative targets set, except in governmental institutions themselves (Dagevos 2001: 90).

The second Purple Coalition government (1999-2002) made an explicit connection between urban and integration policies by instating a Minister for Urban Policies and Integration based in the Ministry of Home Affairs. In this period, Dutch-as-a-second language education became a core activity in a variety of programmes and projects. Again, the objective was to improve the chances people with a minority background had at acquiring jobs on the Dutch labour market. This initiative took the form of offering the long-term unemployed among minority groups (Smeets et al. 1999: 16) internships that promote Dutch language-learning as well as compulsory courses in language and integration (known in Dutch as *'inburgering'*). This trend continued in the successive Balkenende governments. In 2003, Dagevos and Turkenburg observed that there was a tendency to drop specific measures for ethnic minorities, partly because of the rapid decline of unemployment in this group during the second half of 1990s. Dagevos and Turkenburg assumed a certain fatigue also played a role vis-à-vis the specific attention and programmes for ethnic minorities in the labour market policy (Dagevos et al. 2003: 257). Nevertheless, the high youth unemployment remained on the policy (and research) agenda (Dagevos 2006) and, in February 2007, the Social and Economic Council (SER) published updated advice to the government on how to improve the labour market position of ethnic minority youth. SER's recommendations included calling upon different parties in the labour market as well as in the field of education to cooperate and make extra investments to improve the situation of these groups. The council also urged the government to speed up plans to establish a national network of discrimination reporting centres (SER 2007).

5.3 The labour market position of Turks and Moroccans in Amsterdam and Rotterdam

Over the years, Amsterdam's and Rotterdam's economies have grown due to their important roles as ports. Both cities enjoy the reputation of being international centres of trade and commerce, and this has resulted in high percentages of people there employed in the trade and transport sector. However, most people work in the business service sector, namely 23 per cent in Amsterdam and 19 per cent in Rotterdam. In Amsterdam, financial institutions are also important, as 10 per cent of employed people works there.

Data on the working-age population at the city level that distinguish the first from the second generations are available only for the year 2004. Given our interest in the second generation, we have chosen to present these figures in Tables 5.1 and 5.2. Second-generation Turks and Moroccans still form a small part of the working-age population in the two cities, though they have paid work more often than their predecessors in the first generation do. The difference with the comparison group is huge across all age groups, however. Participation in the labour market is lower in Rotterdam in all age and ethnic age groups than in Amsterdam.

Amsterdam and Rotterdam – two of the 'big four' cities, together with The Hague and Utrecht – have the highest share of households with a low income in the country. While 9 per cent of all households in the Netherlands have a low income, 17 per cent of the households in Amsterdam and 16 per cent in Rotterdam are in this unfavourable position. On average, non-western households in Amsterdam are two-and-a-half times more likely to have a low income than households of Dutch

Table 5.1 *Working-age population with paid work in Amsterdam and Rotterdam in %, by age group, ethnic group and generation, 2004*

	Turks		Moroccans		Comparison group
	First generation	Second generation	First generation	Second generation	
Amsterdam					
15-24	41.3	45.1	45.1	48.4	59.2
25-35	51.4	65.9	51.9	63.5	85.3
Total 15-65	42.4	50.7	41.2	51.6	71.6
Rotterdam					
15-24	36.0	38.3	36.7	38.2	62.5
25-35	47.6	61.0	42.0	56.4	84.8
Total 15-65	39.4	44.7	34.7	41.5	68.8

Source: Statistics Netherlands

Table 5.2 *Working-age population with social benefits in Amsterdam and Rotterdam in %, by age group, ethnic group and generation, 2004*

	Turks		Moroccans		Comparison group
	First generation	Second generation	First generation	Second generation	
Amsterdam					
15-24	7.2	5.0	7.4	5.1	3.0
25-35	24.2	21.1	25.2	24.2	17.5
Total 15-65	34.5	9.4	34.4	9.1	7.7
Rotterdam					
15-24	11.5	8.7	14.4	8.5	4.5
25-35	29.0	26.5	35.3	30.9	16.8
Total 15-65	38.8	13.8	41.5	12.6	9.8

Source: Statistics Netherlands

descent. In Rotterdam, the distribution is even more skewed. Non-western households are three times more likely to have a low income than Dutch households. In Amsterdam, about half of the non-western households with a low income depend on the lowest social security benefit known as the *bijstandsuitkering*. In Rotterdam, only 26 per cent of the low-income households have paid work. Some 58 per cent of the non-western households with a low income in Rotterdam receive a *bijstandsuitkering* (Lautenbach & Siermann 2007).

Table 5.2 gives information about dependence on social security benefits in the two cities. Similar to observations of the labour market, the important differences are those between the comparison group and the two foreign descent groups, with the latter more often dependent on social security benefits. In this case, we only find small differences between the two generations of each ethnic group.

5.4 Labour market position of the three study groups in the TIES survey

All TIES respondents were asked whether they were active on the labour market. The comparison group, being older on average, most often had a job or jobs; second-generation Moroccans – being the youngest – were more often still fulltime students, combining a job with studies or following an apprentice track. The different age patterns partly account for the statistically significant differences we find between the ethnic groups, as shown in Table 5.3. The second generation faces higher unemployment than the comparison group, and a significant proportion of women of Turkish descent participate in neither

Table 5.3 *Labour situation, by ethnic group and sex*

	Second generation				Comparison group	
	Turks		Moroccans			
	Men	Women	Men	Women	Men	Women
Has one or more jobs	50.3	36.8	40.4	30.0	57.3	63.2
Has own business	3.5	0.9	1.2	1.5	8.1	0.0
Self-employed	2.2	0.7	0.1	0.4	5.4	2.2
Has job(s) and is in school	14.3	13.6	20.0	25.1	15.0	17.0
Following an apprentice track	6.0	4.9	6.7	7.9	2.1	2.3
Has unpaid family work/family business	0.3	2.3	0.5	0.0	0.8	0.0
Unemployed though not seeking a job	1.0	1.2	2.3	0.5	0.3	0.9
Unemployed and seeking a job	9.6	9.7	9.7	7.1	1.6	1.7
Takes care of children or family	0.0	17.1	0.0	11.5	0.0	3.9
Unable to work (sick or disabled)	2.4	2.9	1.2	2.2	0.7	0.9
Fulltime student without a job	9.2	9.3	16.5	13.8	8.7	7.8
Don't know	1.2	0.5	1.4	0.0	0.0	0.0
Total	100.0	100.0	100.0	100.0	100.0	100.0
N	242	258	246	246	250	262

school nor work because they take care of children or other family members. This scenario is rare below the age of 30 in the comparison group. Second-generation Moroccan women are found to be in an intermediate position when looking at age- and gender-specific patterns.

For the Turkish second generation and the comparison group, differences according to gender are statistically significant. Study is still important for people in the age group of eighteen to 35; however, three out of four respondents reported already having experience with the transition from school or study to the labour market. The transition could be categorised as either temporary, because the individual went back to school after having worked for a while, or more permanent, after having transferred from one job to another.

We asked respondents how many months it took before they found their first job after having finished fulltime schooling, as well as what they did right after school. Table 5.4 gives an overview of the answers. It is interesting to observe that so many found a job right away. This is the case for all ethnic groups, for both men and women, with the comparison group in the most favourable position. While the differences among the three groups overall are statistically significant, within the groups, they are not statistically significant according to sex.

Table 5.4 *Situation after finishing education and before first job, by ethnic group and sex*

	Second generation				Comparison group	
	Turks		Moroccans			
	Men	Women	Men	Women	Men	Women
Did household work	1.9	11.8	2.5	4.1	0.6	1.2
Was unemployed though not seeking a job	7.0	12.3	9.9	10.1	4.4	2.6
Was unemployed though actively seeking a job	27.0	17.7	20.3	18.2	14.7	17.5
Did short-term odd jobs	11.8	13.5	18.6	18.4	20.7	14.8
Helped in the family business without pay	0.5	0.2	0.7	0.5	0.0	0.5
Worked in the family business for pay	2.3	0.2	0.3	1.7	0.7	1.3
Immediately found a job	47.3	44.3	47.2	47.1	58.8	62.1
Performed compulsory army service	2.2	0.0	0.6	0.0	0.0	0.0
Total	100.0	100.0	100.0	100.0	100.0	100.0
N	194	185	179	168	194	199

Only second-generation Turkish women report staying at home and doing household work in substantial numbers, which is in line with earlier observations. Being unemployed and spending a brief period actively looking for work is also found to be relatively evenly spread across groups and gender. The reported time needed to find a first job after finishing fulltime school was, on average, two months; the comparison group had a slightly more favourable position, with an average of 1.7 months, and no differences were reported between men and women. In the second-generation Turkish group, men reported a shorter waiting period than women when it came to finding work, whereas the opposite was found in the second-generation Moroccan group: women report an average of 1.9 months and men, 2.6 months.

Thus, what are the main jobs of the currently employed respondents? And in which sectors of the economy are they active? The Standaard Beroepenclassificatie (the Dutch standard occupational classification 1992, i.e. SBC-92) used to classify the most important job. Table 5.5 gives an overview of job levels by ethnic group, showing that the observable differences are statistically significant. We have chosen to exclude here those currently employed respondents who combine work with study so as not to distort comparisons over the ethnic groups with such respondents' unequal distribution. Given that study and jobs are most often combined in the second-generation Moroccan group, we lose a third of the cases if we confine ourselves to those with work only. In the comparison group, we lose only 18 per cent of the cases. Between

Table 5.5 *SBC* level of current job for those who finished education, by ethnic group*

	Second generation		Comparison group
	Turks	Moroccans	
Elementary	9.8	12.7	4.2
Lower	34.8	34.6	15.0
Secondary	35.9	35.4	26.6
Higher	14.7	15.0	39.2
Scientific	4.8	2.3	15.1
Total	100.0	100.0	100.0
N	206	174	318

* Standaard Beroepenclassificatie 1992

45 and 47 per cent of Turkish and Moroccan second-generation respondents is found in elementary and lower level jobs, and 17 to 19 per cent is found in higher-level jobs. The occupations of the comparison group show another distribution altogether; more than 50 per cent is in higher-level jobs.

The figures in Table 5.5 do not reveal differences between men and women or according to age. By comparing mean occupational prestige values, Tables 5.6a and b shed light on the development of prestige with age (Table 5.6b) and differences in prestige according to gender (Table 5.6a). The Ultee and Sixma occupational prestige ladder (U&S-92) is used to assign scores to all occupations coded in the SBC-92. The U&S-92 scores are measured on an interval scale.

Table 5.6a *Average prestige score (U&S-92) of current jobs for those who have finished education, by ethnic group and sex*

	Second generation				Comparison group	
	Turks		Moroccans			
	Men	Women	Men	Women	Men	Women
Mean	40.4	44.8	37.4	46.0	54.0	53.2
Standard error of mean	2.9	2.9	3.0	3.2	0.9	0.9
N	126	80	98	76	162	156

Table 5.6b *Average prestige score (U&S-92) of current jobs for those who have finished education, by ethnic group and age group*

	Second generation				Comparison group	
	Turks		Moroccans			
	18-24	25+	18-24	25+	18-24	25+
Mean	35.3	46.2	36.7	44.2	42.9	55.8
Standard error of mean	3.0	2.7	3.3	3.0	1.4	0.7
N	76	130	74	100	55	263

Interestingly, women of Turkish and Moroccan descent have higher prestige scores than men of the same ethnic group. This time, the opposite pattern is found for the comparison group, but the differences are very small. While the differences between the three groups are statistically significant, those by sex in each ethnic group are not. With increasing age, one would expect the prestige scores to improve, particularly after the age of 25 (when people most have finished their education). In line with this expectation, we find statistically significantly higher scores with advancing age among young people of Turkish descent and the comparison group. The differences between the groups also increase, particularly between the two second-generation groups and the comparison group.

The sectors in which men and women work differs, too; while there are hardly any second-generation Turkish or Moroccan men found in health care and social work or in education, a third of all women work in these sectors. Men's jobs involve manufacturing, construction and work in the transport sector. The trade and financial sectors attract both men and women of all groups in roughly equal amounts (10 to 15 per cent).

The Netherlands is known for its high proportion of people – and especially women – who work part-time. Do we find this pattern in our young population, too? The general trend is confirmed if we look at the figures by ethnic group and gender (not in table). Around half of the second-generation women and 40 per cent of women in the comparison group have part-time jobs, while six to eight out of ten men work fulltime. If we disaggregate by age, however, differences by gender hold, yet they decrease substantially as age increases. Above the age of 25, half of the second-generation women work more than 32 hours a week.

All respondents with work were asked about their satisfaction in terms of how the level of skills their job required met the skills they had to offer. For the comparison group, the match between the skills required and possessed was quite good: almost 75 per cent felt there was a match (not in table). Consistency between skills required and skills possessed was found for only about half of the second-generation groups. In the second-generation Moroccan group, respondents most often state that they were working below their own perceived level of skills. This held true for men in particular (there is a 10 per cent difference with the women). The fact that the second-generation Moroccan group has the youngest age distribution and the comparison group, the oldest, does play a role here. As with fulltime versus part-time work, the skills required and possessed become more balanced with increasing age.

What are the future plans of those who are currently working? Table 5.7 presents the answers given to the question. It is striking that all of

Table 5.7 *Future plans concerning working career of those who do paid work, by ethnic group and sex*

	Second generation				Comparison group	
	Turks		Moroccans			
	Men	Women	Men	Women	Men	Women
Continue current work	33.5	28.6	24.3	19.1	36.0	30.6
Part-time work/ work fewer hours	1.1	4.4	0.0	2.3	0.0	2.8
Look for promotion/ more challenging job	19.7	20.8	26.7	24.1	38.2	38.4
Start own business	17.0	8.3	20.1	11.6	10.0	8.8
Persue new or additional training	13.7	22.8	20.2	24.7	3.8	8.0
Become fulltime homemaker	0.0	0.7	0.0	0.9	0.0	0.0
Other	15.0	14.3	8.7	17.3	11.9	11.4
Total	100.0	100.0	100.0	100.0	100.0	100.0
N	163	125	147	138	208	211

the groups are quite ambitious, i.e. a substantial number claim that they aim for a promotion, a more challenging job or further education. There are differences between men and women, as men more often say that they want to start their own business. Second-generation Turkish women and women of the comparison group mention wanting to pursue additional training twice as often as their male counterparts. The gender differences are only statistically significant for the comparison group.

There is only a small group of respondents who are unemployed – 8 per cent across groups – though with substantial differences visible between the comparison group and the second-generation groups (see Table 5.3). Because the comparison group is particularly small, with only sixteen unemployed persons, this group is not considered further here. In the second-generation groups, between 10 and 11 per cent are unemployed. Between 83 and 88 per cent of those without a job are looking for work. The unemployed report having been in this position for quite some time already, on average, being ten months since the last paid job. Second-generation Turks seem worse off, with around 60 per cent without paid work for more than six months; for second-generation Moroccans, this is true in 44 per cent of the cases.

Summarising, the picture of the labour market situation has positive and negative aspects that are in line with the general picture. There is more unemployment, and the level of jobs is lower for Turks and Moroccans of the second generation compared with the comparison group. On the positive side, we find a lot of ambition to study and move up, particularly among women of the second-generation groups.

5.5 Income position of the three ethnic groups in the TIES survey

Most of the respondents have some sort of independent income such as through work, a scholarship or a social benefit. Table 5.8 gives an overview of income sources per group. The second-generation Moroccans, being the youngest, most often receive some sort of benefit, which is only the case for 23 per cent of the older, comparison group. For the majority of cases – 75 per cent – this concerns student scholarships in both groups. While slightly less than half of the second-generation Moroccan women have some sort of benefit, for men, the rate is only 35 per cent. These differences are not statistically significant, however. In the other two ethnic groups we do not find gender differences. Those with a scholarship very often still live in their parental home; of those living with their parents, between 82 and 92 per cent have a student scholarship, and this is found across all groups. A conspicuous 10 per cent of second-generation Turks mention receiving a disability benefit, which is three times higher than the rate among second-generation Moroccans and five times higher than the rate in the comparison group.

The survey collected information on the monthly net amount of euros respondents earned. In line with earlier tables, we limit ourselves here to those who have finished school and present net monthly income from employment only. Table 5.9 gives an overall picture across the three groups. The respondents in the comparison group earn quite a bit more than those in the second-generation groups: while almost 65 per cent of the second-generation Moroccans earn below 1,500 euros per month, this is true for only around one-third of those in the comparison group. Only in the comparison group do we find significant differences between men and women. Given the larger numbers and higher position of the comparison group in the labour market, this is no surprise. However, without taking the household situation into account, this is a rather rough first indication. Consistent with analyses in earlier chapters, we have therefore also looked at the income amounts according to living arrangement.

Table 5.8 *Reception of benefits, by ethnic group*

	Second generation		Comparison group
	Turks	Moroccans	
Receives some sort of benefit	33.7	43.9	23.0
Receives no benefits	66.3	56.1	77.0
Total	100.0	100.0	100.0
N	500	492	512

Table 5.9 *Net monthly income from employment for those who finished education, by ethnic group and sex*

	Second generation				Comparison group	
	Turks		Moroccans			
	Men	Women	Men	Women	Men	Women
Less than € 550	4.5	6.2	7.5	12.5	1.6	5.1
Between € 550 and € 999	12.0	21.4	18.3	13.6	8.3	7.4
Between € 1,000 and € 1,499	31.8	42.4	34.8	45.9	19.4	22.6
Between € 1,500 and € 1,999	34.6	14.7	28.7	17.5	26.3	41.2
Between € 2,000 and € 2,499	6.8	1.0	1.6	1.5	23.4	8.9
Between € 2,500 and € 2,999	2.0	3.6	1.2	3.8	8.0	5.7
More than € 3,000	2.8	0.9	0.2	0.0	6.1	2.6
Don't want to say	5.7	7.7	5.0	4.1	5.3	4.5
Don't know	0.0	2.1	2.8	1.2	1.5	2.0
Total	100.0	100.0	100.0	100.0	100.0	100.0
N	133	88	101	84	171	164

Table 5.10 presents information about respondents who live in their own household with a partner (and sometimes with children) and those who live with their parents. These two groups represent about 60 per cent of the respondents and illustrate the differences across groups and situations.

Table 5.10 *Net monthly income from employment, by living arrangement (excluding single-person households) and ethnic group*

	Second generation		Comparison group
	Turks	Moroccans	
Own household with partner (and/or children)			
Less than € 550	3.5	13.4	1.3
Between € 550 and € 999	11.5	8.3	9.3
Between € 1,000 and € 1,499	40.7	44.6	18.9
Between € 1,500 and € 1,999	33.6	28.9	36.6
Between € 2,000 and € 2,499	4.9	2.2	17.1
Between € 2,500 and € 2,999	2.9	2.5	11.1
More than € 3,000	2.8	0.0	5.6
Total	100.0	100.0	100.0
N	115	59	161
In parental/grandparental household			
Less than € 550	8.5	15.2	13.3
Between € 550 and € 999	30.3	22.0	27.3
Between € 1,000 and € 1,499	39.5	40.4	44.3
Between € 1,500 and € 1,999	18.5	21.5	11.4
More than € 2,000	3.2	0.9	3.7
Total	100.0	100.0	100.0
N	54	54	22

LABOUR AND INCOME   99

Respondents with their own household and a partner generally have higher incomes. These individual incomes form just part of the household income, as partners may also be contributing income from work. There are important differences between the ethnic groups as far as the extent to which respondents' partners earn an income. Respondents of the comparison group more often have a partner who has completed their education and earns a job-based income than do second-generation respondents. Partners who contribute to household income generally bring in more money than the respondent if the respondent's income is low to begin with, and about the same if the respondent already earns a relatively good income. Given that partners of comparison group respondents more often work and work for better pay than do partners of second-generation respondents, one can safely conclude that the income situation in the households of the comparison group is much more favourable than that of the second-generation groups.

The lowest net incomes are found among respondents who live with their parents: 18 per cent of the respondents who finished school and have a job live with their parents. Only 16 per cent of them come from the comparison group. This means that roughly one in four respondents of Turkish or Moroccan descent who are no longer in school lives with their parents. The conditions in these parental homes vary greatly across the different groups. Ninety per cent of the fathers of the comparison group and 67 per cent of the mothers have paid work, while this is true for only a third of the Moroccan fathers and 10 per cent of the mothers. Of the Moroccan fathers, 27 per cent is retired and 25 per cent receives a disability benefit. The situation in Turkish parental households is slightly more favourable, with 56 per cent of the fathers and 20 per cent of the mothers having paid work, and dependence on retirement or disability benefits being lower at 31 per cent. Not presented in the table are those respondents who live alone. Although one in five respondents with a job-based income work lives alone, 75 per cent are found in the comparison group. Most of them also have a relatively high income: 68 per cent has an income above 1,500 euros per month.

5.6 Discrimination on the labour market

Discrimination can be a great obstacle for Turks and Moroccans trying to enter the labour market. *Monitor Rassendiscriminatie 2005*, published by the Landelijk Bureau ter bestrijding van Rassendiscriminatie (LBR, National Bureau Against Racial Discrimination), notes that 60 per cent of the people of Moroccan descent and 49 per cent of those of Turkish descent who report irregularities say they felt discriminated against during job interviews at least once in the previous year because of their origin. In comparison, only 2 per cent of the population of Dutch descent who report discrimination attributed it to their origin. On the work floor, a quarter of the people of Turkish and Moroccan descent said they experienced discrimination (Boog et al. 2006). The Netherlands has several laws dealing with discrimination. The most important law is the Algemene Wet Gelijke Behandeling (AWGB, Equal Treatment Act), which came into effect in 1994. People who feel they are treated unequally at work or school and suspect it has to do with their race, religion, gender or political preference can call upon this law (www.cgb.nl/cgb120.php).

In all life domains and in various ways, people may sense and experience open as well as disguised forms of discrimination. What are the experiences of the respondents in our survey regarding hostility and unfair treatment in the labour market? Are there differences found between the three groups, between the two cities and between men and women?

Table 5.11 presents answers, by ethnic group, to the question of perceived discrimination when looking for a job. Between the cities, the two ethnic groups and the two sexes, we do not find statistically significant differences in perceptions, despite the fact that men more often express experiences of unfair treatment. Table 5.12 reports experiences at the workplace for respondents who have a history of jobs.

As in Table 5.11, the differences between men and women are greater than those found between the cities; this time, differences in perceptions between second-generation Moroccan men and women are statistically significant.

Apart from personal experiences of discrimination, we also asked respondents how they perceived entry into the labour market on a group basis for people of Turkish or Moroccan descent compared with people from the comparison group. This question – in a slightly different manner – was asked of the comparison group also, being phrased as fol-

Table 5.11 *Perceived personal discrimination in finding a job, by ethnic group and sex*

	Second generation			
	Turks		Moroccans	
	Men	Women	Men	Women
Never	50.7	56.1	45.2	55.7
Rarely	18.8	18.6	14.3	18.7
Occasionally	22.1	11.9	24.6	13.7
Regularly	3.8	11.2	11.6	6.0
Frequently	4.6	2.2	4.4	5.8
Total	100.0	100.0	100.0	100.0
N	176	139	161	158

Table 5.12 *Perceived personal discrimination at the workplace, by ethnic group and sex*

	Second generation			
	Turks		Moroccans	
	Men	Women	Men	Women
Never	42.0	56.9	46.2	59.1
Rarely	25.6	13.5	17.5	18.5
Occasionally	24.1	21.8	25.0	16.1
Regularly	4.3	6.5	6.3	4.8
Frequently	3.9	1.3	4.9	1.6
Total	100.0	100.0	100.0	100.0
N	189	178	176	159

lows: 'According to you, is it just as difficult, less difficult or more difficult for people of Turkish and Moroccan origin to find a good job than for people of Dutch origin of the same age and qualifications?' The question posed to the second generation was: 'According to you, is it just as difficult, less difficult or more difficult for you to find a good job than for people of Dutch origin of the same age and qualifications?' The three groups have statistically significantly different perceptions on these issues. Table 5.13 presents the results by ethnic group and city.

The second-generation groups in Rotterdam are more negative about the chances their group has on the labour market than are their counterparts in Amsterdam. But these differences by city are not statistically

Table 5.13 *Perceived group discrimination of Turks and Moroccans in finding a job, by ethnic group and city*

	Second generation		
	Turks	Moroccans	Comparison group
Amsterdam			
Much less difficult	1.7	0.8	0.5
Less difficult	7.0	2.8	1.7
As difficult	50.5	47.1	21.8
More difficult	30.4	36.0	68.1
Much more difficult	10.5	13.2	7.8
Total	100.0	100.0	100.0
N	237	241	259
Rotterdam			
Much less difficult	2.4	0.4	0.4
Less difficult	2.5	4.1	2.3
As difficult	40.8	37.4	30.3
More difficult	37.3	42.4	60.8
Much more difficult	17.0	15.8	6.3
Total	100.0	100.0	100.0
N	263	251	253

significant (nor are they by sex). What is most revealing in this table are the views of the comparison group. As many as two-thirds to three-quarters of the comparison group – particularly in Amsterdam – think that people of Turkish and Moroccan origin have much more difficulty finding a good job than do people of Dutch origin. Only in Amsterdam do the perceptions among the three ethnic groups on discrimination of Turks and Moroccans differ in a statistically significant way.

5.7 Conclusions

Amsterdam and Rotterdam have diverse local economies and relatively high proportions of households that face poverty. Households of Turkish and Moroccan descent are among at-risk groups for having low income, due to high unemployment and low participation in the labour market. The first generation – which is three times as big as the second generation – determines the macro-picture of the labour market. Second-generation Turks and Moroccans are still at the beginning of their working life. Between the two ethnic groups and the comparison group a gap prevails, though the second generation is in a better position than the first one. Compared to the first generation, a substantially higher percentage of second-generation Turks and Moroccans in the age group 25 to 35 enjoy paid work in both cities.

The labour market and income situation of the second generation in the TIES survey are consistent with the bigger picture. There is greater unemployment and lower-level jobs for Turks and Moroccans of the second generation than for the comparison group. A real assessment of the extent to which the Dutch labour market offers equal opportunities can be made if future studies can jointly analyse labour and education characteristics. An encouraging result from our survey is that many respondents, particularly women, voiced their ambitions to study and move up the occupational ladder. As the survey showed, when second-generation women have paid jobs, they are employed at an equivalent or better level than men in their ethnic group. Women are also more satisfied with their work in terms of the skill level required. More often than men, they express interest in enhancing their educational level through further or additional training. One in two second-generation women above the age of 25 with a job works fulltime. Compared with the mothers of these women, the difference is huge. Men of the second generation perceive discrimination in the labour market more often than women, both for themselves and for their group. One might argue, though, that women are less exposed to such situations in the labour market than men because of their lower participation rate to begin with.

Lower-level jobs result in lower income, and it is therefore not surprising that respondents of the comparison group have better incomes than the second-generation groups. The fact that the respondents of the comparison group are, on average, four to five years older than members of the two second-generation groups plays an important role in these differences, and one should thus be cautious in interpreting this result. Instead of looking at age-specific figures, we chose to compare respondents in the same household situation. We compared the individual incomes of those with their own household and a partner and the ones who lived with their parents, across ethnic groups. All respondents who live with their parents have the lowest incomes, but it is noteworthy that one in four respondents who have finished school and earn an income lives in the parental home. The income situation is very different in the parental homes of our second-generation respondents than in those of the comparison group. Whereas in the latter group, the majority of the parents both work, this is not the case in Turkish and Moroccan households. These households largely depend on a combination of social security such as retirement, unemployment and disability benefits.

References

Boog, I., J. van Donselaar, D. Houtzager, P. Rodrigues, R. Schriemer, H. van der Berg & J. Evers (2006), *Monitor Rassendiscriminatie 2005*. LBR: Rotterdam.

Dagevos, J. (2001), *Rapportage minderheden 2001. Deel 2. Meer werk*. The Hague: Sociaal en Cultureel Planbureau (SCP publicatie; 2001-17b).

Dagevos, J. (2006), *Hoge (jeugd)werkloosheid onder etnische minderheden: Nieuwe bevindingen uit het LAS-onderzoek*. The Hague: Sociaal en Cultureel Planbureau.

Dagevos, J. & M. Gijsberts (eds.), *Jaarrapport integratie 2007*. The Hague: Sociaal en Cultureel Planbureau (SCP-publicatie; 2007-27).

Dagevos, J., M. Gijsberts & C. van Praag (2003), *Rapportage minderheden 2003: Onderwijs, arbeid en sociaal-culturele integratie*. The Hague: Sociaal en Cultureel Planbureau (SCP-publicatie; 2003-13).

Lautenbach, H. & C. Siermann (2007), 'Armoedeprofielen van de vier grote steden', *Sociaal-economische trends* 1st quarter: 49-57. Voorburg: CBS.

Martens, E. & Y. Weijers (2000), *Integratiemonitor 2000*. Rotterdam: Instituut voor Sociologisch-Economisch Onderzoek (ISEO).

SCP/WODC/CBS (eds.) (2005), *Jaarrapport Integratie 2005*, 57-80. The Hague: SCP/WODC/CBS.

SER (2007), *Niet de afkomst maar de toekomst: Naar een verbetering van de arbeidsmarktpositie van allochtone jongeren*. The Hague: Sociaal-Economische Raad.

Smeets, H., E. Martens & J. Veenman (1999), *Jaarboek minderheden 1999*. Houten: Bohn Stafleu Van Loghum.

Snel, E., M.M.V. Stavenuiter & J.W. Duyvendak (2002), *In de fuik. Turken en Marokkanen in de WAO*. Utrecht: Verwey-Jonker Instituut.

6 Identities and intercultural relations

George Groenewold

6.1 Introduction

While the previous chapters dealt with contextual and structural dimensions of the integration of the second generation, this chapter addresses the socio-cultural dimensions. Specifically, it describes indicators for ethnic and other group identifications as weak as for intercultural relations within Dutch society.

Differences in language, socio-political history, religious notions and symbols have been important factors shaping the diversity in national cultures and identities in European populations. More recently, immigration in larger numbers has added new cultures and identities, contributing to a further diversification. From a socio-cultural and psychological perspective, this set off an 'acculturation process', which means that contact between existing populations and immigrant groups leads to adaptations in the cultural orientations of all groups concerned (Berry 1997; Rummens 2001). Contrary to traditional views (e.g. Gordon 1964), Glazer and Moynihan (1963) argue that cultural pluralism is a more plausible view than presuming that assimilation is the inevitable outcome of immigrant adaptation. This view was later elaborated by Berry (1997), Bourhis et al. (1997) and Navas et al. (2007), who maintain that acculturation should be looked at from a multi-dimensional and multiple life-domain perspective. Thus, persons may pursue different acculturation strategies, thus implying that cultural identity is not 'exclusive': people from different groups may identify with different cultural characteristics according to differing circumstances (Arends-Tóth & Van de Vijver 2001, 2002; Berry 1997; Galchenko et al. 2006; Phalet & Ter Wal, 2004; Phinney et al. 2001; Rudmin 2003; Verkuyten & Tijs 1999; Vedder & Van de Vijver 2003). In the TIES project, 'identity' is therefore defined as a multi-component indicator of feelings and constructions of belonging to different 'groups' and 'communities' (including nations and ethnic communities). Thus, at the conceptual level, identity comprises multiple identities pertaining to different life domains. When it comes to actual TIES survey measurements, this is reflected, for example, by asking about the intensity of respondents' feelings of simultaneous belonging to a variety of identities, including national, ethnic and local ones.

Section 6.2 begins with a narrative describing the Dutch context of identity and intercultural relations. Section 6.3 analyses feelings people express regarding belonging to certain social groups and their identification with Dutch society. As identities are dependent on more aspects than just ethnic origin, the analysis proceeds with other important cultural dimensions of ethnic identity, such as language proficiency and use (section 6.4), religious practices and religiosity (section 6.5) and transnational relations (section 6.6). The chapter concludes with an analysis of views on norms and values, the multicultural society at large and members of other social groups (section 6.7).

6.2 Dutch context of identity and intercultural relations

The idiosyncratic Dutch language is an important element of Dutch identity. So, too, are the norms, values and use of religious symbols and paraphernalia inspired by the Protestant and Catholic religions. The importance that most non-western immigrant groups in the Netherlands give to religion and religiosity warrants a few sentences on the changing importance of religion in the Netherlands. At the time of the country's latest constitutional reform in 1848, almost all Dutch citizens self-affiliated with one of three main religious denominations: Protestant (i.e Dutch Reformed), Calvinist (known as 'Gereformeerd') and Catholic. A mass process of secularisation started in the second half of the nineteenth century and accelerated from the 1960s onwards. By 2002, about 40 per cent of the population did not affiliate with any religion, while 31 per cent was Catholic, 21 per cent was Protestant (14 per cent Dutch Reformed; 7 per cent Calvinist) and 5 per cent was Muslim. In the Netherlands' main cities, the proportion of Dutch people without a religion is somewhat higher. For instance, in the Amsterdam region, 49 per cent are non-religious, while in Rotterdam, this is 59 per cent. Protestants constitute the largest religious denomination in Amsterdam (i.e. 22 per cent), followed by Catholics (14 per cent) and Muslims (10 per cent); in Rotterdam, Catholics constitute the majority (15 per cent) followed by Muslims (13 per cent) and Protestants (9 per cent) (RIVM/CBS 2003).

A study in Rotterdam among ethnic group members between eighteen and 30 years old revealed that 55 per cent of the 'native Dutch' described themselves as not religious at all, while the corresponding figures among Turks and Moroccans are 1 per cent and 0 per cent., respectively In these ethnic groups, 73 per cent and 56 per cent, respectively, reported that they were not actually practising their religion fully, while only about 26 per cent and 44 per cent, respectively, said they followed the precise rules of their religion in daily life. These figures suggest that forms of secularisation among the younger generation of Turks and Moroccans may develop. Other studies reveal that almost all Turks and Moroccans identify with Islam, and, though their active participation in religious ceremonies varied, Islamic norms and practices remain important in domestic life (e.g. raising children, partner choice). Affiliation with Islam appeared stable across generations, while participation in religious ceremonies was lower in the younger generations, notably among better-educated and economically active persons. This suggests an emerging individualisation in the form of a 'Dutch' Islam. These studies also confirm the expected association between religious and ethnic affiliation (Phalet et al. 2000; Phalet & Ter Wal 2004). Among the comparison group, the situation is quite different. Religion as a form of guidance in domestic and public life has lost much of its prominence, similar to the situation elsewhere in Europe.

Policies in the Netherlands over the last ten years have shifted, spurring on more obligations for newcomers. In 1998, a new policy was launched in the form of the Wet Inburgering Nieuwkomers (WIN, Civic Integration [Newcomers] Act). This act meant increased pressure on new immigrants, as the government made mastery of the Dutch language obligatory. Through special mandatory training courses, the government also expected immigrants to learn about the Netherlands' national history as well as the established norms and values of Dutch culture,. After 2000, issues already politicised during and after the rise and fall of Fortuyn's political party led to an increase in restrictive immigration and integration policies. For instance, the WIN policy was extended in 2002 to include *oudkomers* (literally, 'old-comers'), i.e. those who immigrated before the launch of the 1998 WIN policy. Among Turkish and Moroccan *oudkomers*, more than 75 per cent lacked sufficient Dutch language proficiency and other skills to, in the eyes of the government, successfully integrate into Dutch society (the implication being that parents rarely if ever used Dutch to communicate with their children (Erf & Tesser 2001; Tesser & Erf 2001; Tubergen & Kalmijn 2002)).

Problems were traced to the lack of social interaction between ethnic groups. Problems that arose from cultural differences have been attributed by some (e.g. Koopmans 2002) to the failure of adequate policymaking and implementation, while others attribute it to the larger differences between social norms and values underpinning Dutch culture vis-à-vis those maintained by first-generation Turkish and Moroccan immigrants. The authors Van de Brink (2006) and Demant (2005) attest to the latter argument in the case of the Netherlands. They describe how differences in culture-driven attitudinal characteristics of people of

Dutch ancestry vis-à-vis people of Turkish and Moroccan descent affect the socio-cultural integration process in which all three groups participate. For example, it was found that people of Dutch descent scored highest on such values as 'pragmatism' and 'individualism', while people of Turkish and Moroccan descent scored highest on values like 'orthodoxy' and 'group-centeredness'. This finding is consistent with central values underlying Protestant ideology, including the belief in personal autonomy, self-responsibility and meritocracy. Furthermore, from the perspective of social dominance theory, the hierarchy-enhancing Protestant ethic provides moral and intellectual legitimisation of status hierarchy and inequality between ethnic groups, which is difficult to reconcile with the kind of group-thinking and egalitarianism underlying multiculturalism (e.g. see Katz & Hass 1988; Levin et al. 1998; Verkuyten & Brug 2004).

6.3 Indicators of identity

Table 6.1 shows results of a set of similar questions addressing feelings of belonging among the respondents. It describes the degree to which respondents identify with their own ethnic group and other social and spatial entities.

Although percentage distributions are given by ethnic group and by sex, only a few distributions appear to differ in a statistically[1] significant way (i.e. the sex differences in religious identity among comparison group members and sex differences in feelings of being Dutch among members of the second generation).

Figures in Table 6.1 show that about 80 per cent of the second generation hold strong or very strong feelings of belonging to their own ethnic group – which corresponds to similar figures on feelings of 'being Dutch' among the comparison group.

Not surprisingly, the distributions between second-generation Turks and Moroccans differ when it comes to their affiliation with either the Kurdish or Berber cultures, something that is very much influenced by the ethnic origin of their parents. Kurds constitute about 20 per cent of the population in Turkey, and Berbers comprise about 40 per cent of the population of Morocco (Andrews 2002; MEOE 2007). About 14 per cent of second-generation Turkish respondents identify strongly or very strongly with the Kurdish ethnic group, while the figure for the second-generation Moroccans is about 55 per cent.

The largest difference between the second generation and the comparison group is found in relation to religious identity. More than 80 per cent of the respondents identify strongly or very strongly with being Muslim. By contrast, about two-thirds of the comparison group men-

Table 6.1 *Identification of respondents with different types of social and spatial entities, by ethnic group and sex*

			Not at all	Very weak	Weak	Neither weak nor strong	Strong	Very strong	Total	N
Turk	Turks[a]	Men	2.3	0.2	2.0	15.5	31.6	48.6	100.0	196
		Women	0.9	0.9	2.5	20.7	31.1	43.9	100.0	224
Moroccan	Moroccans[b]	Men	0.3	2.6	0.9	9.1	41.7	45.3	100.0	200
		Women	0.4	2.2	5.3	15.6	35.3	41.4	100.0	199
Kurd	Turks	Men	63.8	5.6	9.4	8.8	9.8	2.6	100.0	100
		Women	45.7	14.1	6.6	18.8	6.1	8.8	100.0	99
Berber	Moroccans	Men	22.1	4.5	3.8	11.6	26.3	31.8	100.0	165
		Women	10.3	13.4	6.0	17.9	22.3	30.1	100.0	133
Muslim/ Christian	Turks	Men	1.7	4.3	4.3	10.3	30.2	49.3	100.0	176
		Women	2.5	2.4	1.5	13.5	22.7	57.3	100.0	201
	Moroccans	Men	4.1	1.8	0.8	8.8	29.5	55.0	100.0	195
		Women	1.0	2.6	1.6	10.1	27.9	56.9	100.0	188
	Comparison group	Men	57.8	7.8	8.1	9.9	5.5	10.9	100.0	218
		Women	36.9	11.3	9.6	16.4	10.3	15.5	100.0	241
Dutch	Turks	Men	9.5	5.9	15.4	35.8	28.1	5.3	100.0	191
		Women	4.6	1.8	10.7	39.2	33.9	9.7	100.0	220
	Moroccans	Men	7.3	4.0	12.9	33.8	30.2	11.8	100.0	202
		Women	0.8	5.7	9.1	36.3	30.1	18.1	100.0	209
	Comparison group	Men	0.5	2.1	3.3	18.2	39.1	36.8	100.0	231
		Women	0.3	0.5	2.5	13.1	43.5	40.2	100.0	251
Citizen of Amsterdam/ Rotterdam	Turks	Men	4.3	3.0	3.1	24.2	38.6	26.8	100.0	193
		Women	5.7	2.5	3.2	23.1	38.3	27.3	100.0	215
	Moroccans	Men	2.1	1.2	5.6	15.1	39.1	36.8	100.0	204
		Women	0.8	1.1	3.6	22.2	38.3	33.8	100.0	210
	Comparison group	Men	0.7	2.1	13.2	22.4	31.9	29.7	100.0	228
		Women	1.6	5.1	6.2	25.6	39.7	21.8	100.0	248
European	Turks	Men	13.8	8.0	13.8	28.8	29.5	6.2	100.0	176
		Women	6.2	8.9	8.5	39.6	29.2	7.5	100.0	201
	Moroccans	Men	15.6	9.3	15.9	22.3	31.6	5.4	100.0	195
		Women	6.0	9.3	11.7	38.1	24.2	10.6	100.0	188
	Comparison group	Men	3.6	5.4	14.7	34.3	33.2	8.8	100.0	218
		Women	1.4	4.8	11.8	32.7	40.2	9.0	100.0	241

[a] All instances of 'Turks' in this and other tables in this chapter refer to the second generation.
[b] All instances of 'Moroccans' in this table and other tables in this chapter refer to the second generation.

tion that they have no feelings at all, very weak feelings or weak feelings of belonging to any religion. Both numbers are in accordance with official statistics on religious affiliation and figures found in previous research (RIVM/CBS 2003; Phalet & Ter Wal 2004; Phalet et al. 2000). The high figures reflected in Table 6.1 for ethnic and religious affiliations suggest that they are intertwined; being a second-generation Moroccan (and to a lesser degree, a second-generation Turk) seems to index a 'cultural' reference to being a Muslim (see also below). Another genuine difference is apparent with regard to religious-identity feelings among the comparison group: men more often say that they do *not* have feelings of belonging to any religion.

With regard to feelings of being 'Dutch', about one-third of second-generation Turkish men and almost one-fifth of their female counterparts have weak feelings, very weak feelings or no feelings of belonging at all. Figures for second-generation Moroccans show slightly higher degrees of identification: one in four men and one in seven women identify weak feelings or none at all vis-à-vis feeling Dutch.

Table 6.1 also shows that many of the second generation have strong or very strong feelings of belonging to their respective city – these feelings are even stronger than among the comparison group. The same is true for feelings of belonging to one's neighbourhood of residence (data not shown). This shows that strong feelings of belonging to one's ethnic group do not contradict strong feelings of belonging to the place where people live. The data seem to suggest that the second generation may well combine strong feelings of belonging to their own ethnic group with strong feelings of being Dutch, thus confirming what has been suggested in the literature about persons having multiple identities (e.g. Berry 1997). Although this may be the case, this cannot directly be concluded from the table, seeing as the reported percentages for both identity types may pertain to different respondents.

This issue is further explored in Table 6.2, showing that there is a large proportion of second-generation Turks (38 per cent) and Moroccans (45 per cent) who strongly identify with Islam but *also* identify with the Netherlands. Another 37 per cent of the second-generation Turkish respondents and 34 per cent of the second-generation Moroccan respondents who report a strong identification with Islam indicate that their feelings of belonging to the Netherlands are neither weak nor strong. Thus, relatively more second-generation Moroccans combine a strong identification with Islam with strong feelings of being Dutch.

The bottom panel of Table 6.2 confirms that respondents of the two groups maintain stronger feelings more often for their city of residence than for the Netherlands, per se. Furthermore, it shows that a strong identification with Islam is more easily combined with a local identity than with a national one.

Table 6.2 *Description of feelings of belonging to Islam combined with feelings of belonging to the Netherlands and to Amsterdam or Rotterdam, by ethnic group*

		Strength of feelings of belonging to Islam			
	Strength of feelings of belonging to the Netherlands	Weak	Not strong or weak	Strong	Total
Turks	Weak	18.2	23.5	24.8	24.1
	Not strong or weak	27.3	41.2	37.6	37.2
	Strong	54.5	35.3	37.6	38.7
	Total (N=392)	100.0	100.0	100.0	100.0
	Group distribution	8.0	12.4	79.6	100.0
Moroccans	Weak	11.1	15.4	21.6	20.3
	Not strong or weak	22.2	53.8	33.6	34.8
	Strong	66.7	30.8	44.8	44.9
	Total (N=397)	100.0	100.0	100.0	100.0
	Group distribution	6.5	9.4	84.1	100.0
		Strength of feelings of belonging to Islam			
	Strength of feelings of belonging to Amsterdam/Rotterdam	Weak	Not strong or weak	Strong	Total
Turks	Weak	18.1	17.6	9.3	11.0
	Not strong or weak	27.4	29.4	22.2	23.5
	Strong	54.5	52.9	68.5	65.4
	Total (N=391)	100.0	100.0	100.0	100.0
	Group distribution	9.2	11.5	79.3	100.0
Moroccans	Weak	0.0	15.4	6.8	7.2
	Not strong or weak	12.5	38.5	15.4	17.4
	Strong	87.5	46.2	77.8	75.4
	Total (N=400)	100.0	100.0	100.0	100.0
	Group distribution	6.3	11.3	82.5	100.0

Identity data were also examined from the perspective of whether or not respondents can *simultaneously* identify, whether strongly or very strongly, with different types of identities. Our findings confirm the expectation that people have multiple identities and that identification with one single identity is the exception rather than the rule. Of the six types of identities listed in Table 6.1, second-generation Turks and Moroccans identify, on average, with three, whereas the comparison group identifies with two. The comparison group does have a smaller number of realistic options. These figures are also representative for men and women and for the younger and older cohorts among the respondents, as sex and age group differences appear to be negligible. About 5.9 per cent and 3.9 per cent of the second-generation Turks and Moroccans respondents, respectively, did not identify strongly or very strongly with any of the identities as listed, while the figure for the comparison group is slightly higher (8.9 per cent).

6.4 Language proficiency and use

Proficiency in Dutch as well as in the parental language and use of these languages among peers are other indicators of group identification. As described in section 6.2, the lack of Dutch language skills among first-generation immigrants from Turkey and Morocco has been a major impediment to their successful economic and socio-cultural integration in the Netherlands.

The situation of the second generation is entirely different. Table 6.3 presents the numbers on self-reported proficiency in Dutch and the dominant language in the parents' country of origin. More than 97 per cent of the second-generation Moroccan and Turkish respondents say that they have a good, very good or excellent command of the Dutch language in terms of speaking, reading and writing.

A somewhat different picture emerges when the respondents are asked about their proficiency in Turkish and Moroccan Arabic. At least three of four second-generation Turkish and Moroccan respondents indicate that they speak their mother tongue well, very well or even excellently, while less than 5 per cent of the second-generation Turks and 8 per cent of the second-generation Moroccans say they do not speak the language well. This is not surprising given that 96 per cent of second-generation Turks state that Turkish was the main language used in their upbringing and 71 per cent of second-generation Moroccans state that Moroccan Arabic was used in theirs. The information in Table 6.3 is also given by age and sex. Although the distributions differed slightly, these differences were not statistically significant.

Table 6.3 *Self-reported proficiency in Dutch language and ethnic group language, by ethnic group*

		Poor	Not so good	Moderate	Very good	Good	Excellent	Total	N
Dutch language									
Speaking	Turks	0.0	0.2	2.5	22.4	29.7	45.2	100.0	434
	Moroccans	0.2	0.0	1.2	15.4	26.4	56.7	100.0	409
Reading	Turks	0.2	0.9	1.6	16.6	28.3	52.3	100.0	434
	Moroccans	0.2	0.0	0.7	15.4	19.6	64.1	100.0	409
Writing	Turks	0.7	0.9	3.7	22.1	26.7	45.9	100.0	434
	Moroccans	0.2	0.2	2.0	17.6	24.2	55.7	100.0	409
Ethnic group language									
Speaking	Turks	0.7	4.7	12.7	34.7	27.3	20.0	100.0	433
	Moroccans	4.3	3.6	16.4	35.0	17.9	22.9	100.0	405
Reading	Turks	3.3	6.0	17.2	29.1	21.9	22.5	100.0	433
	Moroccans	28.1	14.4	22.3	18.7	7.2	9.4	100.0	405
Writing	Turks	3.3	11.3	14.7	28.7	22.0	20.0	100.0	433
	Moroccans	33.3	18.1	22.5	13.8	5.8	6.5	100.0	405

IDENTITIES AND INTERCULTURAL RELATIONS 113

Particularly among second-generation Moroccans, some other local languages were also mentioned as being used in upbringing, such as Tamazight (14 per cent), Tashkelhiyt (6 per cent), and Classic Arabic (6 per cent). Among second-generation Turks, the percentage of respondents reporting the use of other languages is negligible (e.g. Kurdish: 2.6 per cent). However, three of four respondents in both groups report that Dutch was also used during their upbringing.

Overall, second-generation Moroccans use the Dutch language more frequently in their communication than do second-generation Turks. More than 90 per cent of the second-generation Moroccans use the Dutch language when speaking with brothers, sisters and friends, while this is the case for only 62 per cent of the second-generation Turks. Slightly more than half of second-generation Moroccans also mention that they predominantly or exclusively speak Dutch with their partner, as opposed to the one-third of second-generation Turks who report those. When it comes to addressing their fathers or mothers, 28 per cent of second-generation Moroccans do so in Dutch, while this is the case for only 13 per cent of second-generation Turks.

6.5 Religion

6.5.1 Affiliation with religion

As shown above, most of the second generation strongly identify with Islam as the predominant religion in their parents' country of origin. Table 6.4 presents a closer look at religious affiliation during childhood and adolescence and confirms that a vast majority of the second generation was raised with Islam. Conversely, almost 60 per cent of comparison group respondents say they were raised without any religion. Most of the respondents raised with a religion are Catholics or Protestants.

Table 6.5 combines information obtained on religious affiliation during upbringing with information on respondents' current affiliations. This may serve as an indicator of secularisation over time. The first two rows indicate people who still have the same status with regard to religious affiliation as they did in their youth. The third row shows that about 5 per cent of the responding second generation went from a religious upbringing to practising secularism. According to the last row, 5 per cent of the second-generation Turks and only 2 per cent of the second-generation Moroccans turned to Islam after coming of age. Gender differences appeared to be small and not statistically significant.

The distributional characteristics of the comparison group in Table 6.5 are consistent with strong general trends in secularisation among the Dutch population (cf. Knippenberg 2004). Not only was more than half of the comparison group raised in a non-religious family, but up to

Table 6.4 *Religious affiliation, by ethnic group*

	Second generation		Comparison group
	Turks	Moroccans	
Raised with religion	88.2	92.7	41.2
Not raised with religion	11.8	7.3	58.8
Total	100.0	100.0	100.0
Raised as:			
Christian: Catholic	0.9	0.9	45.8
Christian: Protestant	0.6	0.3	43.9
Christian: Orthodox	0.3	0.0	0.0
Christian: Other	0.3	0.2	6.0
Muslim: Sunna	41.3	44.0	1.3
Muslim: Shia	0.8	0.7	0.0
Muslim: Alevi	6.8	0.8	0.0
Muslim: Other	48.5	52.3	0.4
Jewish	0.0	0.0	0.3
Other	0.6	0.8	2.3
Total	100.0	100.0	100.0
N	439	425	483

Table 6.5 *Secularisation trends and differentials: religious affiliation during upbringing and current status, by ethnic group*

Religious affiliation		Turks	Moroccans	Comparison group
During youth	Currently			
No	No	7.3	6.3	55.7
Yes	Yes	83.3	86.7	15.7
Yes	No	4.9	4.9	27.9
No	Yes	4.6	2.1	0.7
Total		100.0	100.0	100.0
N		439	425	483

20 per cent of those raised religiously no longer have religious affiliations. This does not necessarily mean that all are non-believers. By contrast, the secularisation trend among the second generation seems very small.

6.5.2 Religiosity

Studies revealed that, despite variation in active participation in religious ceremonies, Islamic norms and values remain important in domestic life (e.g. child-raising and partner choice). Affiliation with Islam appears stable across generations, while the actual participation in ceremonies is lower among younger generations, notably among better-educated and economically active persons. This seems to suggest an emerging individualisation in 'Dutch practices' of Islam. The bulk of studies on secularisation shows that figures reflecting religious affiliation should not be taken as measures of religiosity, for changes in religiosity necessarily precede changes in the religious affiliation, mainly because of conformation to peer-group pressure (cf. Knippenberg 2004). This is complicated by the above-mentioned fact: there is an association between religious and ethnic affiliation (cf. Table 6.10 below; Phalet et al. 2000; Phalet & Ter Wal 2004).

In the survey, respondents were asked about their attendance of religious services in a mosque, a church or some other place of worship (excluding social festivities or funerals that might take place therein) and the frequency of daily prayers. Responses to these types of behavioural questions should be interpreted with care because they tend to solicit 'socially correct' answers. Among respondents who stated having a religion, the same proportion of second-generation Turks and Moroccans – one in ten – said they pay a weekly (or more frequent) visit to the mosque. Among the comparison group, visiting a place of worship is more common, as one in four respondents stated they visited their church on a weekly (or more frequent) basis.

About half of the religious second generation say that they never, or rarely if that, visit a mosque, while the figure is significantly lower (about one-third) in the comparison group. It should be noted again that the group of practising Christians in the age range of eighteen to 35 is quite selective because it represents only 16 per cent of male and 22 per cent of female comparison group members. Second-generation women more often than men say they seldom or never visit a mosque: while this applied to 65 per cent of the second-generation women we surveyed, it was the case for only about 40 per cent of their male counterparts. Not surprisingly, only a small proportion (6 per cent) of Turkish and Moroccan women mention visiting a mosque once a week or more often. Age differences within each of the three groups regarding attendance frequency are not statistically significant.

Asking about praying frequency may be more informative, though it is a methodologically problematic question because it invites socially desirable answers. About half of all second-generation Moroccans state that they pray according to the sequence of prayers required by the Koran, which involves praying five or more times each day. This practice is done by only one in ten second-generation Turks, while four in ten even reported that they never pray at all. A considerably smaller proportion of second-generation Moroccans (26 per cent) said that they do not pray at all. Within each group, significant differences by sex and by age are absent. In addition to these behavioural indicators of religiosity, respondents who stated having a religion were also asked to what extent they agree or disagree with a number of statements on the role religion plays in personal life. The results are presented in Table 6.6.

The most striking finding is, again, the contrast between the comparison group and the second-generation groups. For the second generation, the role religion plays in personal life is much greater than for the predominantly 'ethnic Dutch' respondents. In general, second-generation Moroccans more often hold firmer positive attitudes towards the importance of religion in their lives than second-generation Turks do, although only the second, third and fourth items show statistically significant differences between the two groups.

Table 6.6 *Perceptions on importance of religion in personal life, by ethnic group*

	Being a (Muslim, Christian, other religion) is an important part of myself						
	Totally agree	Agree	Neither agree nor disagree	Disagree	Totally disagree	Total	N
Turks	48.5	34.1	11.4	3.8	2.3	100.0	380
Moroccans	48.5	34.9	3.9	2.3	0.8	100.0	376
Comparison group	21.9	31.6	19.3	23.5	3.7	100.0	87
	The fact that I am a (Muslim, Christian, other religion) is something I often think about						
	Totally agree	Agree	Neither agree nor disagree	Disagree	Totally disagree	Total	N
Turks	25.6	34.6	18.8	15.8	5.3	100.0	379
Moroccans	41.4	37.5	10.9	6.3	3.9	100.0	373
Comparison group	18.2	25.7	17.1	31.0	8.0	100.0	87
	I see myself as a real (Muslim, Christian, other religion)						
	Totally agree	Agree	Neither agree nor disagree	Disagree	Totally disagree	Total	N
Turks	22.9	35.1	32.1	8.4	1.5	100.0	378
Moroccans	36.7	35.9	23.4	2.3	1.6	100.0	372
Comparison group	11.8	24.2	23.7	34.9	5.4	100.0	87
	In many aspects I am like other (Muslims, Christians, other religion)						
	Totally agree	Agree	Neither agree nor disagree	Disagree	Totally disagree	Total	N
Turks	12.3	41.5	29.2	12.3	4.6	100.0	377
Moroccans	19.4	43.4	27.9	8.5	0.8	100.0	375
Comparison group	5.9	37.4	27.8	26.2	2.7	100.0	87
	When somebody says something bad about my religion I feel personally hurt						
	Totally agree	Agree	Neither agree nor disagree	Disagree	Totally disagree	Total	N
Turks	31.3	33.6	16.8	14.5	3.8	100.0	379
Moroccans	27.7	35.4	20.0	10.8	6.2	100.0	374
Comparison group	5.9	22.6	13.4	46.2	11.8	100.0	87

IDENTITIES AND INTERCULTURAL RELATIONS

Within each of these groups, age and gender differences were examined, but the differences are slight and mostly insignificant, though with one exception: within each of the three groups, the younger cohorts more often feel personally hurt when something bad is said about their religion.

Finally, the questionnaire contained another set of statements on the more general role and importance of religion in society and the use of religious symbols in public life. Table 6.7 below presents the results.

Table 6.7 *Perceptions on role of religion in wider society and importance given to the use of religious symbols outside the home, by ethnic group*

	Religion should be a private matter between a religious person and God						
	Totally agree	Agree	Neither agree nor disagree	Disagree	Totally disagree	Total	N
Turks	47.0	32.5	13.2	6.6	0.7	100.0	437
Moroccans	37.7	37.7	15.1	5.5	4.1	100.0	425
Comparison group	32.0	44.7	14.1	8.9	0.4	100.0	483
	Religion should be represented in politics and society, along with other religious or political viewpoints						
	Totally agree	Agree	Neither agree nor disagree	Disagree	Totally disagree	Total	N
Turks	4.6	20.5	34.4	27.2	13.2	100.0	436
Moroccans	6.8	21.9	36.3	19.9	15.1	100.0	423
Comparison group	2.0	14.6	23.0	34.0	26.4	100.0	483
	Religion should be the only and ultimate political authority						
	Totally agree	Agree	Neither agree nor disagree	Disagree	Totally disagree	Total	N
Turks	2.6	9.9	31.1	30.5	25.8	100.0	436
Moroccans	3.4	8.2	30.1	31.5	26.7	100.0	421
Comparison group	0.5	0.5	6.1	19.2	73.7	100.0	483
	All religious symbols or signs should be banned from schools						
	Totally agree	Agree	Neither agree nor disagree	Disagree	Totally disagree	Total	N
Turks	4.6	10.5	23.0	34.2	27.6	100.0	437
Moroccans	2.7	6.8	17.1	33.6	39.7	100.0	425
Comparison group	5.5	6.6	18.5	54.5	14.9	100.0	483
	Islamic women should wear headscarves or cover their heads outside the house						
	Totally agree	Agree	Neither agree nor disagree	Disagree	Totally disagree	Total	N
Turks	10.1	10.7	35.6	21.5	22.1	100.0	436
Moroccans	13.7	16.4	36.3	19.2	14.4	100.0	424
Comparison group	6.8	10.9	22.2	46.8	13.3	100.0	483

The first and probably most interesting outcome is that, in all groups, a vast majority (around 80 per cent) agrees that religion should be a private matter between an individual and God. The only outstanding result among the groups in this aspect is that the position is strongest among second-generation Turks. This is bolstered by the relatively low proportion of respondents in favour of religion as 'the only and ultimate political authority', which is around 12 per cent in both second-generation groups.

Most of the items listed in Table 6.7 address issues that are common subjects in public debate. As a result, individual preferences or viewpoints may be biased towards one of the popular positions held in recurrent public debates on these issues. The question about whether Islamic women should cover their heads outside the house, for example, may be interpreted either as reflecting personal beliefs and preferences or deferring to some popular position in the public debate regarding freedom of belief or the role of women in Islam. This may explain why the number of respondents opting for the extreme answer categories 'totally agree' or 'totally disagree' in most item questions is very low and why most respondents opted for the middle category 'neither agree nor disagree'. However, the combined responses of some item questions do exhibit a much wider spectrum of positions, such as the one on 'religion as the ultimate political authority'. Almost 60 per cent of the second generation and about 90 per cent of the comparison group position themselves in the categories 'disagree' or 'totally disagree', while more than 60 per cent of respondents in all three groups choose firm positions in their rejection of laicism.

Regarding the representation of religion in politics and society 'along with other religious or political viewpoints', answers for the second-generation groups are clustered around the central position. The question garners neither clear agreement nor disagreement, which may be because of the many diverse connotations that the statement may arouse. Here, only the comparison group shows higher percentages of respondents who 'totally disagree' with the statement that religion should be represented in politics and society. This is consistent with the over 90 per cent rate of rejecting religion as the only acceptable political authority.

It is somewhat complicated to drawing firm conclusions about people's endorsement or rejection of the wearing of headscarves by Muslim women outside the house. While a majority of the comparison group (60 per cent) is against it, there is also a non-negligible percentage (18 per cent) in favour of it. The latter percentage is only slightly less than that observed among the Turkish second generation (21 per cent) and considerably less than that among second-generation Moroccans (30 per cent). And still, a considerable group of almost 45 per cent

IDENTITIES AND INTERCULTURAL RELATIONS   119

of second-generation Turks and Moroccans reject the wearing of headscarves by Muslim women outside the house.

This question was also examined from a gender and age perspective. Only among members of the comparison group were statistically significant differences by sex found, as men more often than women expressed stronger opinions on the issues addressed. Differences by age are small, notably among the second generation, and younger cohorts more often tend to cluster in the middle category of 'neither agree nor disagree'.

6.6 Transnationalism

Another way of looking at the identification of the second generation is by examining different types of linkages to their parents' country of origin. This can be done through looking at their exposure to Turkish or Moroccan media, examining visitation behaviour to Turkey and Morocco and seeing whether the second generation sends remittances to, or invests in, these countries. Such practices would be indicative of a transnational lifestyle orientation among the second generation.

It is assumed that the three groups we surveyed have equal access to watching Dutch-, Turkish- and Moroccan-language TV channels. Most cable TV and home-satellite systems in Rotterdam and Amsterdam provide this access. Generally, the frequency and intensity of watching TV reflect no real difference between the three groups: about 97 per cent of the respondents, irrespective of age and sex, watch TV 'every now and then'. With regard to the choice of TV channels, about 37 per cent of the second-generation Turks mainly or exclusively watch Dutch-language channels, and an additional 39 per cent watches both Dutch- and Turkish-language channels. Second-generation Moroccans are much more inclined towards Dutch-language channels, as 83 per cent mainly or exclusively watches Dutch-language channels and only 11 per cent watches Moroccan-language channels.

Second-generation Turks and Moroccans make frequent and periodic visits to their parents' country of origin. About nine out of ten second-generation respondents replied that they visited Turkey or Morocco an average of five to six times in the past five years. Main reasons were 'vacation' (60 per cent) and 'family visits' (37 per cent). These figures represent figures for women and men and for both age groups; statistically significant differentials are absent.

Remitting money or investing in property or business in Turkey and Morocco is not something to be overlooked. An average of about 31 per cent of the second-generation Turks and 25 per cent of the second-generation Moroccans say that they remitted money to their parents' country of origin which includes reference to the tradition of remitting money on certain Islamic holidays. About 65 per cent say that the amount remitted was less than 500 euros per year, while another 15 per cent reported an amount between 500 and 1,000 euros per year. Only a very small proportion, about 5 per cent, of the second generation says that they actually invested money or bought property in those countries. The fairly small number of cases involved prevents a meaningful statistical analysis to examine sex and age differences.

6.7 Intercultural relations

6.7.1 Preferred norms and values

The survey posed four opinion questions to the respondents regarding whether people of immigrant origin should observe norms and values of the majority society or those of their own ethnic group inside or outside the home. Table 6.8 shows the percentage distributions of the response categories.

About eight of ten respondents in each group studied agree or fully agree that, *at home,* people of immigrant origin have the right to live as

Table 6.8 *Perceptions regarding whether people of immigrant origin have the right to live as much as possible in accordance with the cultural customs and norms of their country of origin or the Netherlands, by ethnic group*

		Totally agree	Agree	Neither agree nor disagree	Disagree	Totally disagree	Total	N
At home:								
Own group norms and customs	Turks	43.7	37.7	13.2	3.3	2.0	100.0	434
	Moroccans	49.0	35.4	12.2	2.7	0.7	100.0	425
	Comparison group	25.8	53.5	12.9	6.2	1.6	100.0	483
Dutch norms and customs	Turks	4.0	17.3	28.7	29.3	20.7	100.0	434
	Moroccans	3.4	21.9	21.9	30.1	22.6	100.0	425
	Comparison group	3.2	17.0	25.6	45.5	8.6	100.0	483
Outside home:								
Own group norms and customs	Turks	12.7	30.7	36.7	16.0	4.0	100.0	434
	Moroccans	11.6	31.3	33.3	19.7	4.1	100.0	425
	Comparison group	2.2	15.3	24.1	46.9	11.4	100.0	483
Dutch norms and customs	Turks	9.5	33.1	37.2	13.5	6.8	100.0	431
	Moroccans	9.6	42.5	30.8	12.3	4.8	100.0	422
	Comparison group	19.4	46.6	21.4	10.6	2.0	100.0	493

IDENTITIES AND INTERCULTURAL RELATIONS

much as possible according to the norms and customs of their own ethnic group. However, about one in five second-generation Turks and comparison group members as well as one in four second-generation Moroccans also believe that persons of immigrant origin should live at home according to Dutch norms and customs as much as possible. Although opinions on how to act outside the home are less pronounced, about 43 per cent of the second generation agrees or fully agrees with the statement that immigrants should have the right to live as much as possible according to the norms and customs of their own ethnic group. This is quite different from the views held by almost 60 per cent of the comparison group.

A considerable share of the second-generation Turks (43 per cent) and Moroccans (52 per cent) also perceive that people of immigrant origin should live as much as possible according to *Dutch* norms and customs outside the home. While 85 per cent of respondents of all groups are clear about desirable behaviour inside the home, notable group differences emerge when desirable behaviour outside the home is considered. Interestingly, Turkish and Moroccan respondents adhere in similar degrees to *both* options. Together with high rates for the 'neither agree nor disagree' reply, this may indicate the explanation: '... it depends on the specific situation outside the home...'.

6.7.2 Views on the multicultural society

Respondents were also asked about their opinions on different aspects of living in a multicultural environment. The findings summarised in Table 6.9 shows that second-generation Turks are the most positive about the quality of current relations between Turks and Dutch, as about 60 per cent perceive relations to be friendly, while this is 50 per cent among second-generation Moroccans. Members of the comparison group in the same neighbourhoods are less enthusiastic about relations with people of Turkish or Moroccan descent, as only about 40 per cent describe relations as friendly, or they are indifferent (46 per cent). A few second-generation Turks (10 per cent) and comparison group members (11 per cent) qualify relations as 'not friendly', while this number is somewhat higher for second-generation Moroccans (18 per cent). Gender and age differentials are slight, as are differences between the two cities.

When asked about the *development* of relations between the Dutch and people of Turkish or Moroccan origins, the views of the Moroccan second generation stand out. Almost 60 per cent perceive relations as having become 'less friendly'. Second-generation Turks and the comparison group are much less negative, though one-third in both groups still believes that relations have become less friendly. Views of men and wo-

Table 6.9 *Perceptions on the multicultural society, by ethnic group*

	Quality of current relationship between Dutch and members of Turkish/Moroccan ethnic groups in Amsterdam/Rotterdam					
	Not friendly	Indifferent	Friendly	Don't know	Total	N
Turks	10.0	26.7	60.0	3.3	100.0	434
Moroccans	18.4	31.2	46.8	3.5	100.0	410
Comparison group	11.4	47.0	39.7	1.9	100.0	329
	Development of relationship between Dutch and members of Turkish/Moroccan ethnic groups in recent years in Amsterdam/Rotterdam					
	Less friendly	Same	More friendly	Don't know	Total	N
Turks	30.2	30.9	30.9	8.1	100.0	433
Moroccans	56.7	22.7	14.9	5.7	100.0	411
Comparison group	36.3	35.8	20.2	7.8	100.0	329
	Opinion about the consequences for one's own culture resulting from people of different origins living together in Amsterdam/Rotterdam					
	Threatening	No difference	Enriching	Don't know	Total	N
Turks	9.3	42.4	33.1	15.2	100.0	437
Moroccans	10.9	36.1	44.9	8.2	100.0	425
Comparison group	15.9	29.1	51.9	3.1	100.0	481
	Opinion about whether it is good or bad for the city economy that there are people who originate from different countries living together					
	Not good	No difference	Good	Don't know	Total	N
Turks	8.6	35.1	39.1	17.2	100.0	437
Moroccans	4.8	32.2	51.4	11.6	100.0	426
Comparison group	14.4	36.0	37.7	11.9	100.0	483
	Agreement with the statement that it is good that people of different religions live together in Amsterdam/Rotterdam					
	Agree	Neither agree nor disagree	Disagree	Don't know	Total	N
Turks	48.3	21.2	9.9	20.5	100.0	436
Moroccans	71.2	13.0	6.2	9.6	100.0	425
Comparison group	52.6	27.5	15.1	4.7	100.0	484

men, irrespective of age, are alike, but second-generation Moroccans in Amsterdam (60 per cent) believe that relations have become less friendly more often than their ethnic peers in Rotterdam (51 per cent). This view may reflect recent rising tensions between second-generation Moroccans and other groups connected to incidents of violence.

With regard to the question of whether the presence of other cultures is enriching or threatening for one's own culture, a major difference between the comparison groups in the two cities is found. While 64 per cent of such respondents in Amsterdam emphasise 'enrichment', this applies to only 35 per cent of such respondents in Rotterdam. Only one in ten comparison group members in Amsterdam perceive other cultures as a 'threat', while it is one in four in Rotterdam. Differences in the opinions of men and women, as well as by age, are negligibly small.

When specified for religion, the views respondents had of people with different religions living together in their city are generally positive, which is remarkable in light of recent media attention and concerns about religious extremism. Over 70 per cent of second-generation Moroccans consider it good that people with different religions live together in the same city, while about half of second-generation Turks and the comparison group share that opinion. Only 10 to 15 per cent of second-generation Turks and members of the comparison group believe that it is not such a good idea to have people of different religions living together in the same city. Men and women have more or less comparable opinions on the matter. However, second-generation Moroccans and comparison group respondents in Amsterdam (76 and 63 per cent, respectively) express more often that it is 'good' that people of different religions live together in the same city than members of the same groups in Rotterdam do (62 and 39 per cent, respectively).

6.7.3 Views on members of other ethnic and social groups

Respondents were also asked to rate their feelings about different groups in the society on a 'thermometer scale' ranging from 0 degrees (very negative feelings) to 100 degrees (very positive feelings), with 50 degrees indicating a neutral position. Table 6.10 presents average temperature ratings given by members of the three groups.

In line with expectations, members of the three study groups have similar and positive feelings towards members of their own ethnic group (i.e. 73 or 74 degrees). In the case of the two second-generation groups, this is connected to a generally positive attitude towards Muslims, which is consistent with the above findings about the role of Islam in ethnic group identification for the second generation. The finding that

Table 6.10 *Rating of feelings towards other social groups on a thermometer scale (0-100°), by ethnic group*

	Comparison group	Turks	Moroccans	Blacks/people of darker skin colour	Muslims	Christians	N
Turks	64°	73°	44°	59°	73°	58°	433
Moroccans	69°	64°	74°	69°	80°	69°	422
Comparison group	73°	58°	48°	62°	49°	59°	482

positive feelings towards members of other ethnic groups are generally lower was also expected. However, second-generation Turks and Moroccans have the same degree of positive feelings towards the ethnic Dutch majority population, which is 64 to 69 degrees.

The average rating of feelings towards Muslim in the comparison group in both cities is about neutral (49 degrees), being perhaps slightly negative. Second-generation Turks (58 degrees) and members of the comparison group (59 degrees) have equal and somewhat positive feelings towards Christians. Interestingly, second-generation Moroccans are significantly more positive towards Christians than second-generation Turks. Although feelings towards Blacks or people with a darker skin in general, as the survey so categorised, are generally positive, second-generation Moroccans express positive feelings more often than second-generation Turks and members of the comparison group. Among all the groups, Moroccans are rated the lowest by second-generation Turks and members of the comparison group.

The above results are consistent with the predominantly negative image of the Moroccan ethnic group in the current socio-political climate. Overall, the ratings in Table 6.10 are located between 'neutral' and moderately 'positive'.

Differences according to age and sex are generally small and negligible. The only meaningful difference was observed in age groups of the comparison group, with the younger cohort of respondents between eighteen and 24 years old more often expressing negative feelings towards Moroccans and Muslims than members of the older cohort, in the range of 25 to 35 years old.

6.8 Conclusions

This chapter addressed aspects of identity and issues of intercultural relations. Analysis of the survey data reveals that both second-generation Turks and Moroccans strongly identify with their ethnic group and with Islam as an integral part of ethnic self-definition. This is not to say that there is no identification with the wider society, though both second-generation groups identify more with their city of residence than with the Netherlands or Dutch culture at large. Their strength of city identification is comparable to that of the comparison group. Respondents from the comparison group unsurprisingly identify more often with being Dutch because for them it is also an 'ethnic reference'. Overall, second-generation Moroccans more often exhibit a stronger identification with their own ethnic group, religion and city than do second-generation Turks. But, at the same time, they identify more strongly towards Dutch culture compared with second-generation Turks, in the sense of using Dutch as the primary language for communication (even within their families, as their proficiency in the language of their parents is lower), watching Dutch-language TV and positively evaluating Dutch customs and norms.

Findings show that respondents identify *simultaneously*, albeit it to different extents of intensity, with various life domains, though the second generation does this even more so than members of the comparison group. This provides support for the thesis presented in the introduction of this chapter that identity is a multi-component indicator of feelings and constructions of belonging to different 'groups' and 'communities'.

The degree of 'transnationalism' was examined by analysing data on visits to the country of origin of the parents and the amount of remittances to and investment in that country. Almost all second-generation respondents have relations with their parents' country of origin in the sense that they frequently visit that country, on average once per year. Second-generation Turks more often remit money to Turkey. Only a small fraction has also invested money or bought property in Turkey or Morocco.

Results show that the rapid secularisation among people of Dutch ancestry is not evident (yet) among second-generation Moroccans and Turks. The figures show that only a small proportion raised with Islam does not currently affiliate any longer with that religion. Feelings or religiosity are generally stronger among second-generation Moroccans than among second-generation Turks, and far stronger than in the comparison group. Regarding the role of religion in society, a vast majority of the respondents in all groups agree that religion should be primarily a private relationship between the individual and God.

Views on the 'multicultural society' are predominantly positive in all three groups, though stronger among second-generation Turks and Moroccans. However, the trend in the developments in Dutch society is seen as less optimistic, especially among second-generation Moroccans. In light of various negative socio-political events in recent years, this is probably not surprising. Moroccans are also the lesser positively rated group among members of the Turkish and the comparison group. Most respondents of the comparison group state that other cultures enrich Dutch society, while the second generation is less in support of this. And a majority of all respondents feel positive about people of different religions living together in the same city.

Note

1   Non-parametric tests for ordinal data were used.

References

Andrews, P.A. (2002), *Ethnic groups in the Republic of Turkey, Beiheft Nr. B 60, Tübinger Atlas des Vorderen Orients*, second edition. Wiesbaden: Reichert Publications.

Arends-Tóth, J.V. & F.J.R. Van de Vijver (2001), 'Het belang van acculturatie voor organisaties'. *Gedrag & Organisatie*, 14(2): 55-65.

Arends-Tóth, J. & F. J. R. Van De Vijver (2002), 'Multiculturalism and acculturation: views of Dutch and Turkish-Dutch'. *European Journal of Social Psychology* 33(2): 249-266.

Berry, J.W. (1997), 'Immigration, acculturation, and adaptation', *Applied Psychology: An International Review* 46: 5-68.

Bourhis, R.Y., L.C. Moise, S. Perreault & S. Senecal (1997), 'Towards an interactive acculturation model: A social psychological approach', *International Journal of Psychology* 32 (6): 369-386.

Brink van de, G. (2006), *Culturele contrasten: Het verhaal van de migranten in Rotterdam*. Amsterdam: Bert Bakker.

Demant, F. (2005), 'Meer inpassing dan aanpassing. Over culturele integratie van migranten in Nederland en Duitsland', *Migrantenstudies* 21(2): 70-86.

Erf, R. & P. Tesser (2001), 'Migranten op cursus: Behoefte van oudkomers aan meer kennis van Nederlandse taal en samenleving in kaart gebracht', *Demos* 17(3).

Galchenko, I.V., F.J.R. van de Vijver & E.A. Kirillova (2006), 'Acculturation: Conceptualization and assessment', *Journal of Social Psychology (Russia)*: 3-27.

Glazer, N. & D. P. Moynihan (1963), *Beyond the melting pot*. Cambridge: MIT Press.

Gordon, M.M. (1964), *Assimilation in American life*. New York: Oxford University Press.

Katz, I. & R.G. Hass (1988), 'Racial ambivalence and American value conflict: Correlational and priming studies of dual cognitive structures', *Journal of Personality and Social Psychology* 55: 893-905.

Knippenberg, H. (2004), 'Secularization in the Netherlands in its historical and geographical dimensions', *GeoJournal* 45(3): 209-220.

Koopmans, R. (2002), 'Zachte heelmeesters.....Een vergelijking van de resultaten van het Nederlandse and Duitse integratiebeleid en wat de WRR daaruit niet concludeert', *Migrantenstudies* 18(2): 087-092.

Levin, S., J. Sidanius, J. L. Rabinowitz & C. Federico (1998), 'Ethnic identity, legitimizing ideologies, and social status: A matter of ideological asymmetry', *Political Psychology* 19: 373-404.

Microsoft Encarta Online Encyclopedia (MEOE) (2007), *Berber*, http://uk.encarta.msn.com.

Navas M., A.J. Rojas, M. Garcia & P. Pumares (2007), 'Acculturation strategies and attitudes according to the Relative Acculturation Extended Model (RAEM): The perspectives of natives versus immigrants', *International Journal of Intercultural Relations* 31: 67-86.

Phalet, K. & J. ter Wal (2004), *Moslim in Nederland* (part studies a, b, c and summary). The Hague: SCP-Ercomer.

Phalet, K., C. van Lotringen & H. Entzinger (2000), *Islam in de multiculturele samenleving. Opvattingen van jongeren in Rotterdam*. Utrecht: European Research Centre on Migration and Ethnic Minorities (IMES).

Phinney, J., G. Horenczyk, K. Liebkind & P. Vedder (2001), 'Ethnic identity, immigration, and well-being: interactional perspective', *Journal of Social Issues* 57: 493-510.

RIVM/CBS (2003), *Nationale Atlas Volksgezondheid: Religies in Nederland 2000-2003 per Corop gebied*. Bilthoven.

Rudmin, F.W. (2003), 'Critical history of the acculturation psychology of assimilation, separation, integration, and marginalization', *Review of General Psychology* 7: 3-37.

Rummens, J.A. (2001), *Canadian Identities: An Interdisciplinary Overview of Canadian Research on Identity*. Research report. Halifax: Department of Canadian Heritage.
Tesser, P. & R. van der Erf (2001), 'Oudkomers in beeld. De schatting van een mogelijke doelgroep', Werkdocument 71. The Hague: Sociaal en Cultureel Planbureau.
Tubergen van, F. & M. Kalmijn (2002), 'Tweede taalverwerving en taalgebruik onder Turkse en Marokkaanse immigranten in Nederland: investering of gelegenheid?', *Migrantenstudies* 18(3): 156-177.
Vedder, P. & F.J.R. van de Vijver (2003), 'De acculturatie and adaptie van migrantenjongeren in Nederland: Een vergelijkende studie', *Migrantenstudies* 19(4): 252-265.
Verkuyten, M. & P. Brug (2004), 'Multiculturalism and group status: The role of ethnic identification, group essentialism, and protestant ethic', *European Journal of Social Psychology* 34: 647-661.
Verkuyten, M. & J. Thijs (1999), 'Nederlandse en Turkse jongeren over multiculturalisme; Cultuurbehoud, Aanpassing, Identificatie en Groepsdiscriminatie', *Sociologische Gids* 46: 407-425.

7 Social relations

Liesbeth Heering and Susan ter Bekke

7.1 Introduction

The aim of this chapter is to shed light on the social relations maintained by second-generation Turks and Moroccans and the comparison group respondents. Section 7.2 discusses friendships at secondary school as well as current friendships with members of their own and other ethnic groups. Section 7.3 analyses those organisations in the public domain in which respondents reported being active during the past year. We also examine the extent to which the organisations are oriented towards one's own ethnic group or not. Perceptions about inter-group relations and discrimination are the central issue in section 7.4, while conclusions are presented in section 7.5.

7.2 Ethnic character of friendships in secondary school and at present

Friendships are made in all phases of life, and very often the foundations for long-term friendships are built in school. Respondents in the TIES survey were asked a number of questions about their three best friends at two different stages of their life: during secondary school and at the time of the survey. By comparing these two situations, we assess the extent to which changes have occurred over respondents' lifetimes.

Given the diverse ethnic composition of the populations in Amsterdam and Rotterdam, one might expect that the ethnic background of secondary school friends of second-generation Turks and Moroccans and comparison group respondents would also be diverse. However, this is not the case, as Table 7.1 shows. In particular, the comparison group says that most or all of their three best friends at secondary school were of one ethnic group, in this case, being their own ethnic group. One has to bear in mind that the majority of the comparison group respondents did not live in Amsterdam or Rotterdam when they were in secondary school, and their schools were thus not ethnically mixed (see chapter 4). So the chances of meeting – not to mention in engaging in friendships with – children of Turkish or Moroccan descent

Table 7.1 *Ethnic diversity in best friends at secondary school, by ethnic group*

	Second generation		Comparison group
	Turks	Moroccans	
Same ethnic group	66.1	57.7	92.2
Turkish friends	52.9	0.2	0.1
Moroccan friends	4.8	42.1	0.3
Dutch friends	9.6	15.4	91.9
Diverse ethnic group	31.6	40.3	7.6
Still at school	1.2	0.9	0.0
Don't know	1.2	1.2	0.1
Total	100.0	100.0	100.0
N	433	425	483

were much smaller for the comparison group than the second-generation groups. Best friends at secondary school among second-generation Turks and Moroccans had a more diverse ethnic background; 32 per cent of the second-generation Turks and 40 per cent of the second-generation Moroccans mention three different ethnic groups for their three best friends during this time. Two in three second-generation Turks say their best friends at secondary school were of one or two ethnic groups, however. Second-generation women – particularly, Moroccan women – more often had best friends from the comparison group than did second-generation men, though the differences are not statistically significant. We further examined to what extent the second-generation Turks and Moroccans differ vis-à-vis their friendships with comparison group members. Second-generation Moroccans more often have Dutch friends than second-generation Turks.

Besides asking questions about ethnic and educational backgrounds of their best friends, we also asked how many Dutch friends the second-generation Turks and Moroccans had in secondary school. In the same vein, the comparison group was asked how many Turkish and Moroccan friends they had during that period of life. Combined, the 'none' and 'a few' were given as answers by four in ten second-generation Turks and three in ten second-generation Moroccans (Table 7.2). The answer 'some' was most often given in response to this question, indicating that friendships across ethnic groups are not the rule but the exception. Eighty per cent of the comparison group says that they had 'none' to 'a few' Turkish and Moroccan friends in this period of their lives.

Almost all of the respondents had already left secondary school. For those over 25 years old, this particular period was quite some time ago. We thus asked the same series of questions about people's best friends at the time of the survey. In order to see the differences between the composition of friends over time, we focus on the diversity of best

Table 7.2 *Number of Dutch friends at secondary school among second-generation Turks and Moroccans and number of Turkish and Moroccan friends at secondary school among comparison group members*

	Second generation		Comparison group
	Turks	Moroccans	
None	17.5	14.9	59.7
Very few	25.3	18.6	20.2
Some	35.1	38.6	14.4
Many	13.7	18.0	2.2
Most	8.1	9.0	3.3
Don't know	0.3	0.9	0.1
Total	100.0	100.0	100.0
N	433	422	484

friends at present for those who were no longer in secondary school and compare it with the ethnic diversity of best friends at secondary school. As Table 7.3 shows, the ethnic composition has not changed very much for the second-generation groups.

For these two groups, we find that there are more friendships with members of their own ethnic group at present than in the secondary school period, so the diversity has lessened a bit. The second-generation Moroccan group still engages most in friendships across ethnic boundaries. One in three mentions three different ethnic origins for their three best friends. Among the comparison group, we see the opposite trend: 89 per cent currently has best friends from one or, at most, two ethnic groups, whereas in secondary school, the rate was 92 per cent (Table 7.1). Interestingly, we see that comparison group men have a diverse group of friends more often than comparison group women (13 versus 9 per cent, respectively, not in table). In their diverse groups of friends, ethnicities other than Turkish and Moroccan were also mentioned.

Table 7.3 *Ethnic diversity in current best friends, by ethnic group*

	Second generation		Comparison group
	Turks	Moroccans	
Same ethnic group	73.9	65.4	89.1
Turkish friends	63.5	0.5	0.8
Moroccan friends	2.4	53.9	0.5
Dutch friends	7.9	11.0	87.8
Diverse ethnic group	23.7	33.2	10.6
Don't know	2.5	1.4	0.3
Total	100.0	100.0	100.0
N	437	424	483

Table 7.4 *Number of current Dutch friends among second-generation Turks and Moroccans and number of current Turkish and Moroccan friends among comparison group members*

	Second generation		
	Turks	Moroccans	Comparison group
None	17.1	15.2	57.9
Very few	24.8	24.3	20.8
Some	36.5	37.2	16.1
Many	16.8	17.3	2.5
Most	4.4	5.5	2.6
Don't know	0.4	0.7	0.1
Total	100.0	100.0	100.0
N	439	426	484

Regarding the secondary school period, we asked second-generation Turks and Moroccans how many Dutch friends they had at present, and conversely, we asked the comparison group how many Turkish and Moroccan friends they had at present (Table 7.4). We found that second-generation Moroccans had fewer Dutch friendships at the time of the survey than they did in secondary school. The comparison group was still the group least engaged in friendships with people of Turkish or Moroccan descent. Only about 5 per cent of the comparison group members indicated that *many or most* of their friends are of Turkish or Moroccan descent, and here we find very little difference between men and women for the two answer categories combined.

Concluding, we see that friendships are, to a large extent, confined to one's own ethnic group. The results of Entzinger and Dourleijn on the ethnicity of friendships of youngsters in Rotterdam are similar to ours (Entzinger & Dourleijn 2008: 63-65). The comparison group has the least contact with 'others', while the Moroccan group has the most. It is only in the comparison group that men mention having cross-ethnic friendships more often than women, and only in this group are the differences statistically significant.

7.3 Participation in and ethnic orientation of social organisations

The second aspect of social relations that we examined was respondents' participation in organisations in the public domain of their city. We presented respondents with a list of organisations such as sport clubs, student unions, religious organisations, community organizations and human rights groups, and asked them to identify which ones they undertook activities in over the past year. Table 7.5 gives an over-

Table 7.5 *Number of organisations (maximum of 9) in which activities were undertaken over the past year, by ethnic group and city*

	Second generation				Comparison group	
	Turks		Moroccans			
	Amsterdam	Rotterdam	Amsterdam	Rotterdam	Amsterdam	Rotterdam
0	43.0	49.1	40.8	46.2	22.4	41.7
1	30.6	29.3	37.5	27.7	31.3	33.6
2	12.5	12.8	11.8	16.9	28.3	14.1
3+	13.9	8.8	9.9	9.1	18.1	10.7
Total	100.0	100.0	100.0	100.0	100.0	100.0
N	237	261	242	251	259	253

view of the number of organisations in which respondents undertook activities. In general, participation in such organisations is low. More than 40 per cent of the second-generation Turks and Moroccans did not participate in any organisation at all. Given that many study or combine study with jobs – particularly among the Moroccan group – it is possible that only limited time is left to engage in social activities. The comparison group members, being older and more often in a stable position in terms of school, work and family life, are more active in the public domain, with almost 70 per cent participating in one or more organisations. In Amsterdam, all ethnic groups are more active than in Rotterdam, and the differences in participation between the ethnic groups are significant only in Amsterdam. In the Moroccan group the women are more active, whereas in the Turkish group, we find the opposite: men are more often active outside the home. Differences in participation by gender are, however, not statistically significant.

Apart from the kind and the number of organisations, we also looked into whether activities for each organisation were mostly oriented towards their own ethnic group or not. Table 7.6 lists the top three most popular organisations and shows whether or not there was an ethnic orientation in the organisation or its activities. Sports clubs, which are mentioned most often by the respondents, are, in general, not explicitly oriented to one's own ethnic group. Religious organisations, by contrast, often are. Second-generation Turks are more active than second-generation Moroccans in sports clubs, arts, music or cultural activities and religious organisations, which is in line with what we find in the literature. We find gender differences within the two groups: men are more active in sports clubs or teams, while women are more active in organisations that involve art, music or cultural activities, though all these differences are not statistically significant.

Table 7.6 *Top three organisations in which activities were undertaken by second-generation Turks and Moroccans and whether or not they are oriented towards their own ethnic group*

	Second generation	
	Turks	Moroccans
Sports club or team		
No	72.2	82.4
Yes	27.8	17.6
Total	100.0	100.0
N	198	199
Arts, music or cultural activities		
No	45.7	67.4
Yes	54.3	32.6
Total	100.0	100.0
N	81	47
Religious organisations		
No	29.8	15.5
Yes	70.2	84.5
Total	100.0	100.0
N	54	40

7.4 Perceptions on personal and group discrimination

A third and final feature of social relations has to do with perceptions of discrimination in the different ethnic groups. By first reporting on the work of others on these issues, we intend to put the perception data we collected in their temporal and geographical context. The presentation of our own data starts with the personal experiences respondents have with hostility or unfair treatment, followed by the perceptions of discrimination of all kinds of groups in society. We explored and analysed perceived discrimination by gender and city.

The Social and Cultural Planning Bureau (SCP) collects data on opinions and attitudes regarding the multicultural society on a regular basis. The survey 'Culturele veranderingen in Nederland' (CV) on cultural changes in the Netherlands is one example. Another source of data is the tele-panel survey 'Beeldvorming over minderheden' (BOM) that looks at image-building with respect to minorities. In the 2003 report on ethnic minorities issued by SCP, Van Praag described the opinions and attitudes of different ethnic groups towards each other, relying on the two data sources just mentioned. The data were collected in 2001 after 9/11 and again around the time of the murder of Pim Fortuyn in 2002 (Van Praag 2003: 363). The analysis comparing the opinions of the indigenous population towards people of foreign descent over the decade 1991-2002 shows that the former have become more hostile towards the latter.

From a time perspective of 25 years of CV opinion data on hostility and discrimination, the conclusion is different, however: between 1981 and 2006 there is a significant decrease in perceptions of discrimination (Gijsberts & Vervoort 2007). These results are in line with reports by Entzinger and Dourleijn comparing 1999 and 2006 data on perceived personal and group discrimination by and of ethnic minorities, as collected among immigrant and comparison group members between eighteen and 30 years old in Rotterdam (Entzinger & Dourleijn 2008: 78).

The survey 'Leefsituatie allochtone stedelingen' (LAS) on the living conditions of city-dwellers of foreign descent started in 2004 during the week Theo van Gogh was murdered by a young man of Moroccan descent in Amsterdam. Van Gogh was a well-known moviemaker who made the film *Submission* (part 1) together with Ayaan Hirsi Ali. All respondents of the LAS survey were asked for their opinion on the murder's influence on the relationship between Muslims and non-Muslims in Dutch society. A clear majority of the respondents – irrespective of their own descent – felt that the murder had affected the relationship. Only a minority indicated that their own thinking had changed. A small minority – primarily respondents of Moroccan descent – said that their own lives, as well as those of their families, had been affected by the event (Gijsberts 2005: 202).

Table 7.7 presents the results of our survey by ethnic group with respect to personal experiences of hostility and discrimination. Of both second-generation groups, 45 per cent says they have personally experienced hostility or unfair treatment because of their ethnic background at least once. Of the comparison group, 19 per cent says they have experienced discrimination. For all three groups we found that more men than women claim to have experienced discrimination, though these differences are not statistically significant. There are no significant city differences on this issue either.

Apart from general questions on experiences with discrimination, we also asked respondents about the extent to which they experienced hos-

Table 7.7 *Personal experience with discrimination, by ethnic group*

	Second generation		Comparison group
	Turks	Moroccans	
Yes	44.8	44.8	19.3
No	55.2	55.2	80.7
Total	100.0	100.0	100.0
N	439	426	482

tility or unfair treatment in particular situations. Four situations were presented: in the neighbourhood where respondents live, while going out (in cafes, restaurants and discotheques), in dealings with governmental organisations such as the municipality and in dealings with the police.

The top three situations, ordered from 'most often' to 'least often' in terms of personally experienced hostility, are listed in Table 7.8. Here men and women are distinguished, because the differences by gender outweigh those by group and city. Men experience discrimination more often than women. The overall level of personally experienced hostility is low, with around 60 per cent answering that they never to rarely experienced hostility or unfair treatment. Both second-generation Turks and Moroccans most often experienced discrimination while going out and least often in their own neighbourhood. Second-generation Moroccans, especially, express having frequently or regularly experienced discrimination while going out: almost one in five has felt discriminated against while going out at least once, while this is only the case for one

Table 7.8 *Top three situations of experiencing personal discrimination, by ethnic group and sex*

	Second generation				Comparison group	
	Turks		Moroccans			
	Men	Women	Men	Women	Men	Women
Going out						
Never	28.7	57.8	30.4	59.0	47.9	56.2
Rarely	17.6	27.6	17.7	22.6	30.8	26.1
Occasionally	32.2	13.6	18.8	13.7	18.5	15.6
Regularly	11.0	0.8	16.8	4.5	1.9	1.0
Frequently	10.4	0.2	16.3	0.2	1.0	1.0
Total	100.0	100.0	100.0	100.0	100.0	100.0
N	200	232	209	211	228	252
Encounters with police						
Never	53.0	78.8	51.1	78.1	79.5	89.2
Rarely	16.4	13.5	13.0	10.1	15.7	8.0
Occasionally	15.6	5.6	20.8	6.9	4.0	2.6
Regularly	5.6	1.7	5.6	2.2	0.5	0.0
Frequently	9.4	0.5	9.6	2.7	0.4	0.2
Total	100.0	100.0	100.0	100.0	100.0	100.0
N	201	233	209	212	226	252
Contact with authorities						
Never	52.0	59.1	58.3	65.3	83.0	82.2
Rarely	27.9	19.2	24.7	21.3	10.3	12.2
Occasionally	12.9	18.1	10.1	11.2	5.1	4.2
Regularly	2.0	2.9	3.6	2.2	0.6	0.5
Frequently	5.2	0.7	3.2	0.0	1.0	0.9
Total	100.0	100.0	100.0	100.0	100.0	100.0
N	203	235	209	213	226	252

in ten second-generation Turks. These differences are not statistically significant, though the ones between men and women in each second-generation group are.

In encounters with the police, all women experience discrimination less often than men, though in contact with governmental organisations, the gender differences are not statistically significant.

Experiences in Amsterdam and Rotterdam are different, however, for a few situations. When it comes to encounters with the police and contact with governmental organisations, comparison group members in Rotterdam more often experience discrimination than those in Amsterdam (statistically significant, not in table). In Amsterdam, second-generation Moroccan and comparison group women feel discriminated against less often in encounters with the police than their male counterparts, while this is not significantly so for second-generation Turks. In Rotterdam, second-generation Turkish and comparison group women experience less discrimination in encounters with the police than men do, while these gender differences are not significant for the Moroccan group.

To determine a hierarchy of discrimination of groups, all respondents were asked how often they thought particular groups experienced hostility or unfair treatment because of their origin or background. The groups listed were as follows: Muslims, Turks, Moroccans, Blacks/people with darker skin in general and Dutch people. As Table 7.9 shows, all respondents think the number one group in society to most often experience discrimination is Muslims. The second-generation groups think Muslims experience discrimination frequently; half of the second-generation Moroccans and four of ten second-generation Turks believe this is the case. Of the comparison group one in three thinks Muslims experience discrimination frequently, and only a small proportion thinks that this group is never discriminated against. In Amsterdam, more respondents think Muslims are frequently discriminated against than in Rotterdam. However, only for the comparison group are the differences in opinions by city statistically significant.

The second group in society most often perceived to experience discrimination is Moroccans. Compared with the second-generation Turks, among which six out of ten think Moroccans are regularly or frequently discriminated against, a larger proportion of the comparison group (eight out of ten) and the second-generation Moroccans themselves (almost seven out of ten) think the same. The differences between the cities reveal that a larger proportion of all ethnic groups living in Amsterdam than those in Rotterdam think that Moroccans are regularly or frequently discriminated against. Concerning the Moroccan group, we also find that the city and gender differences are statistically significant only for the comparison group. The third group in the discrimination hierar-

Table 7.9 *Top three groups in society that are perceived to be discriminated against, by ethnic group and city*

	Second generation				Comparison group	
	Turks		Moroccans			
	Amsterdam	Rotterdam	Amsterdam	Rotterdam	Amsterdam	Rotterdam
Muslims						
Never	10.7	11.5	7.8	6.3	1.5	2.8
Rarely	3.0	3.9	4.8	3.8	3.0	2.4
Occasionally	13.5	12.9	8.3	16.8	17.2	16.1
Regularly	24.7	25.3	19.7	25.2	35.4	45.2
Frequently	42.9	41.6	54.0	46.4	38.9	27.6
Don't know	5.2	4.8	5.5	1.5	4.0	6.0
Total	100.0	100.0	100.0	100.0	100.0	100.0
N	203	230	197	225	248	232
Moroccans						
Never	9.4	11.6	7.7	8.4	0.7	1.3
Rarely	2.2	4.8	4.8	6.5	3.4	4.5
Occasionally	13.4	20.6	11.8	19.2	13.9	15.7
Regularly	30.3	28.9	34.3	33.4	39.8	51.0
Frequently	36.6	27.0	37.5	29.6	39.1	22.4
Don't know	8.0	7.1	3.8	3.0	3.2	5.1
Total	100.0	100.0	100.0	100.0	100.0	100.0
N	202	228	197	225	248	232
Turks						
Never	9.6	14.4	8.0	7.6	2.4	2.1
Rarely	8.2	10.3	9.4	8.3	4.9	5.2
Occasionally	40.8	34.9	26.2	29.2	28.3	28.2
Regularly	22.7	24.6	32.7	33.4	48.7	49.1
Frequently	12.0	11.2	16.4	15.1	12.6	10.3
Don't know	6.7	4.7	7.3	6.4	3.2	5.1
Total	100.0	100.0	100.0	100.0	100.0	100.0
N	202	227	196	225	248	232

chy is the Turkish group. In this case, we see that second-generation Moroccans and comparison group members have a different perception of discrimination against Turks than the second-generation Turks themselves have. More comparison group members (six out of ten) and second-generation Moroccans (five out of ten) think Turks are regularly or frequently discriminated against, while only four in ten second-generation Turks perceive the situation this way. More second-generation Turks in Rotterdam than in Amsterdam believe Turks never or rarely experience discrimination, though the city difference is not statistically significant.

Perceived discrimination of groups is clearly different from people's personal experience. On an individual level, few second-generation have perceived being personally discriminated against, though, as a group, they think their ethnicity is subject to more discrimination than the Turkish. Second-generation Turks also feel that their group is discriminated against more often than they personally are, at least in experiences up until the time of the survey.

The situations in which discrimination most often takes place were also analysed. All respondents were asked how often they thought people of Turkish and Moroccan origin experience hostility or unfair treatment in six different situations: at school, at the workplace, when looking for work, when going out, in their neighbourhood and in encounters with the police. The top three situations in which Turks and Moroccans were believed to experience discrimination are found in Table 7.10. The table presents the situations in order from most often mentioned to least often mentioned. Given that the city and gender dimensions did not lead to significant differences in the analysis, we present results by ethnic group.

Table 7.10 *Top three situations in which Turks and Moroccans are perceived to be discriminated against, by ethnic group*

	Second generation		Comparison group
	Turks	Moroccans	
Looking for job			
Never	6.9	4.7	1.8
Rarely	8.6	9.2	5.1
Occasionally	22.8	15.6	23.8
Regularly	30.6	30.3	44.6
Frequently	31.1	40.1	24.6
Total	100.0	100.0	100.0
N	430	418	470
Going out			
Never	9.0	5.4	1.4
Rarely	13.7	8.8	4.6
Occasionally	30.0	18.8	30.8
Regularly	22.4	30.5	39.9
Frequently	24.8	36.6	23.3
Total	100.0	100.0	100.0
N	422	418	468
At work			
Never	9.5	10.7	2.6
Rarely	15.0	13.6	18.1
Occasionally	41.1	39.7	46.4
Regularly	22.5	21.5	26.6
Frequently	11.8	14.4	6.3
Total	100.0	100.0	100.0
N	430	417	466

Three in ten second-generation Turks and four in ten second-generation Moroccans say that their ethnic groups frequently experience unfair treatment or hostility when looking for a job, whereas almost one in four comparison group members say this is the case. We find that more second-generation Turks and Moroccans than comparison group members say that their ethnic group never experiences discrimination when looking for a job.

The number two situation for occurrences of discrimination is identified as taking place while going out. Almost seven out of ten second-generation Moroccans and six out of ten comparison group members think this happens on a regular or frequent basis. More than two of ten second-generation Turks believe this is never or rarely the case.

The number three situation is identified as being at the workplace. For all three groups, a little over 30 per cent believe discrimination of Turks and Moroccans at work happens regularly or frequently. Looking only at the 'frequently' scores, we see that there are somewhat more second-generation Moroccans and Turks giving this answer than the comparison group. One out of ten second-generation Turks and Moroccans says, however, that their ethnic group is never discriminated against at work.

Second-generation Turks and Moroccans are generally more negative about the discrimination against their groups than the comparison group, especially with respect to the primary situation in the discrimination hierarchy: when looking for jobs. Interestingly, the opinions with respect to discrimination at the workplace are much less negative.

7.5 Conclusions

Ethnic orientation in social relations and perceptions of discrimination against ethnic groups in various situations were the two central themes of this chapter. Two aspects of social relations have been explored: the ethnic composition of friendships and the activities and ethnic orientation of social organisations in the public domain in which respondents were active. The gender and city dimensions were always explicitly taken into account in our analyses.

Friendships are, to a large extent, ethnically confined to one's own group. The comparison group has the least contact with members from other ethnic groups, while the Moroccan group has the most. In the comparison group, men mention having cross-ethnic friendships more often than women. Second-generation Moroccans most often mention having Dutch friends. The Turkish group is more oriented towards their own group than the Moroccan group, both in friendships and in the social organisations in which they participate. In Amsterdam, respondents of all three groups are more active in social organisations than in Rotterdam.

Muslims are viewed by all respondents as being the object of hostility and are therefore most often perceived as a group that is discriminated against, which is consistent with the results discussed in the previous chapter and demonstrated by other studies. We found differences in perceptions by city, though only for the comparison group. Comparison group members in Amsterdam more often than their counterparts in Rotterdam have the feeling that Muslims and people of Moroccan descent are discriminated against. With respect to personal experiences of hostility, the gender differences are the most significant. Men have personal experiences with discrimination more often than women.

The Moroccan group is in an awkward, if not paradoxical, situation in that they are the most integrated group at the personal and the societal levels. More than the second-generation Turks, they engage in interethnic friendships and are less oriented towards their own ethnic group as far as their activities in social organisations. At the same time, these investments and ties are not rewarded in the public domain. On the contrary, due to the tense national climate and deviant behaviour of a small group of young male Moroccans, their ethnic group as a whole is negatively stereotyped.

References

Entzinger, H. & E. Dourleijn (2008), *De lat steeds hoger. De leefwereld van jongeren in een multi-etnische stad.* Assen: Van Gorcum.

Gijsberts, M. (2005), 'Opvattingen van autochtonen en allochtonen over de multi-etnische samenleving' in SCP/WODC/CBS (ed.), *Jaarrapport Integratie 2005*, 189-205. The Hague: SCP/WODC/CBS.

Gijsberts, M & M. Vervoort (2007), 'Wederzijdse beeldvorming', in Dagevos, J. & M. Gijsberts (eds.), *Jaarrapport integratie 2007*. The Hague: Sociaal en Cultureel Planbureau (SCP-publicatie; 2007-27).

Praag, C. Van (2003), 'Wederzijdse beeldvorming' in J. Dagevos, M. Gijsberts & C. van Praag (2003), *Rapportage minderheden 2003: Onderwijs, arbeid en sociaal-culturele integratie*, 363-392. The Hague: Sociaal en Cultureel Planbureau (SCP-publicatie; 2003-13).

8 Union and family formation

Helga de Valk

8.1 Introduction

Union formation and partner choice of the second generation are highly debated topics. It is often assumed that union formation among children of immigrants follows more traditional lines than is the case for Dutch young adults. How choices are made and how the factors of influence differ between the second generation and the comparison group are, however, still largely unexplored. The TIES survey provides information on partners living in the same household as the respondents.

This chapter gives an initial descriptive overview of findings on union and family formation. We start by questioning how many young adults live with a partner, what type of union they have and how they met their partners. Secondly, we focus on the role families may play in the partner choice process. Finally, we study family formation and task divisions within the household among young adults from the second generation and those of Dutch origin.

8.2 The context of union and family formation among immigrants

The largest share of non-western immigrants settling in the Netherlands comes to join family (also known as family reunification) or to cohabit with a partner already residing in the Netherlands (also known as family formation). Although family reunification used to be one of the main reasons immigrants came to the Netherlands, since 1997, the number of people settling in the country under this premise has decreased. From 2000 onwards, the number of immigrants arriving in the Netherlands for family formation has come to exceed the number of those coming for family reunification; in 2004 there were twice as many family formation immigrants than those of family reunification (Garssen & Wageveld 2007).

Immigration to the Netherlands is restricted in different ways, and its legislation is laid down in the 2001 Aliens Act. In principle, people can immigrate on the basis of work, family reunification, family formation and asylum seeking. The Dutch government pursues a strict immigration policy regarding family reunification and family formation. Legislation with respect to the latter is based on the internationally accepted right to pursue and maintain a family life. The person applying for family reunification or family formation must meet certain criteria in terms of age and a long-term means of income, factors that were redefined in 2004. In order to apply for family formation nowadays, both partners must be at least 21 years old (eighteen for family reunification). In addition, the couple must be married or have a registered partnership. To be able to acquire a residence permit and settle in the Netherlands, all immigrants (except asylum seekers) between the ages of sixteen and 65 need an authorisation for temporary stay known as a Machtiging tot Voorlopig Verblijf (MVV). Nationals from certain countries (such as EU member states and the US) are waived from this requirement (IND 2007). As of 15 March 2006, all individuals wanting to live in the Netherlands for a longer period will also have to take (and pass) the civic integration examination abroad (IND 2006). Knowledge of the Dutch language and Dutch society is tested by means of an exam, to be taken at the Dutch embassy or consulate in the country of origin. There are substantial costs involved in taking the exam (350 euros) and securing the residence permit (IND 2008).

In general, people tend to marry within their own ethnic group. Looking at the marriages conducted in 2003, this is most clearly the case for people of Turkish and Moroccan descent in the Netherlands: only one in fifteen women from these groups married a person of Dutch descent. The share of marriages with Dutch persons is substantially higher for Surinamese and Antillean women: one in three and one in two, respectively, married a partner of Dutch descent (Garssen & Wageveld 2007; see also De Valk et al. 2001). Recent data from Statistics Netherlands show that second-generation Turks and Moroccans do not marry a Dutch partner any more often than do the first generation. For example, 86 per cent of both first- and second-generation Turkish men married a Turkish woman in 2003. The Surinamese and Antillean second generation are more likely to marry a Dutch partner than the first generation. At the same time, it is clear that Turkish and Moroccan second-generation members choose a partner from their parents' country of origin less often than do members of the first generation. Of those getting married in 2006, between 63 and 71 per cent of second-generation Turkish and Moroccan men chose a partner already living in the Netherlands from their same group of origin. Overall, the figures for 2006 showed that more Turkish men than Moroccan men brought over their partner from the parents' country of origin; 17 versus 9 per cent, respectively (Van Huis 2007).

First-generation Turkish and Moroccan women in the Netherlands started family formation at an earlier age and had more children than did women of Dutch descent. The Total Fertility Rate (TFR) of Turkish women has clearly decreased in the past decennia. The current first-generation Turkish women (who mainly came to the Netherlands for family formation) still have their children at a relatively young age, and teenage (meaning under age twenty) pregnancies are rather common (though the majority of these women is married). The Turkish second generation clearly postpones childbearing, and the age at first birth among this group is getting closer to that of women of Dutch descent. Similar patterns are also found for first- and second-generation Moroccan women. Childbearing is also postponed among Moroccan women, and the fertility of the second generation has especially declined (even more so than among Turkish women). Like women of Dutch descent, many second-generation Moroccan women in their thirties are childless (Garssen & Nicolaas 2006).

8.3 Union formation among the TIES respondents: timing and type of current relationships

The first part of the descriptive analyses on union formation focuses on the percentage of young adults who currently have a partner who is a member of the household. This can be a married or an unmarried partner. Table 8.1 provides an overview, by sex, of the percentages of young adults who have a partner. Almost half of the second-generation Turks and young adults from the comparison group currently have a partner who is a member of their household. The percentage seems to be lower for the Moroccan second generation, of whom 22 per cent report having a partner. When we distinguish between three age groups, 18-24, 25-29 and 30-35, we find that the Moroccan second generation is least likely to have a partner in any of these age groups (not in table). Differences between them and the other two groups are, however, most pronounced in the youngest age group; 8 per cent of the second-generation Moroccans between eighteen and 24 have a partner, as compared with 20 per cent of the second-generation Turks and young adults of the comparison group in this age category. Among the two oldest age groups, we find similarities between the percentages of those with a partner (between 50 and 60 per cent) for second-generation Moroccans and those of the comparison group. At the same time, we find that three-quarters of the Turkish second generation aged 25 or older has a partner. Further multivariate analyses (not in table) also reveal that the apparent differences between the groups are largely attributable to the younger age structure of the Moroccan respondents in the TIES survey.

Table 8.1 *Young adults living with or without a partner in the same household, by ethnic group and sex*

	Second generation				Comparison group	
	Turks		Moroccans			
	Men	Women	Men	Women	Men	Women
With partner in same household	42.9	51.1	14.4	29.4	46.0	45.0
Without partner in same household	57.1	48.9	85.6	70.6	54.0	55.0
Total	100.0	100.0	100.0	100.0	100.0	100.0
N	242	258	246	247	250	262

When we control for the age of the respondents, we find that the likelihood of Moroccan respondents having a partner does not differ from that for the comparison group, whereas the second-generation Turkish respondents are somewhat more likely to have a partner.

Finally, Table 8.1 shows that there are no sex differences in the comparison group when it comes to chances of having a partner. Women of the second generation, by contrast, are more likely to be in a union than are second-generation men.

In line with findings of the share of young adults with partners, we find that second-generation Turks were the youngest group to start living with their current partners (Table 8.2): they were, on average, 21.8 years old, while their Moroccan counterparts were, on average, 22.6 years old. The comparison group was clearly older with an average age of 25.3 years, though the difference is not significantly different from second-generation Moroccan men. In addition, we find that, among the groups, women are younger than men when they start living with a

Table 8.2 *Mean age and age difference between partners when starting to live with current partner, by ethnic group and sex*

	Second generation				Comparison group	
	Turks		Moroccans			
	Men	Women	Men	Women	Men	Women
Mean age living together	22.8	20.9	24.6	21.6	25.6	25.0
Standard deviation	3.1	2.9	2.8	3.1	3.9	4.0
N	93	127	36	76	105	114
Mean age difference between partners*	1.9	-3.6	2.9	-6.6	0.7	-2.8
Standard deviation	2.2	3.7	3.3	3.4	2.9	4.0
N	24	44	20	23	51	55

* Positive values indicate respondent being older than partner; negative values indicate respondent being younger than partner.

partner. This finding is consistent with what we found regarding women's tendency to leave the home at an earlier age and start a union. Sex differences in the mean age are the smallest for the comparison group. For the second generation, men were clearly older than women when starting to live with a partner: two years older in the case of Turkish respondents and three years among Moroccan respondents.

The second part of Table 8.2 provides insight into the age difference between partners for those respondents who reported their partners' age at the start of their cohabitation. In line with what is known from the literature, men are generally older when they start living with a partner. Age differences are the smallest among the comparison group and the largest for the Moroccan couples.

Beside the ages at which partners started to cohabit, the TIES data include information on the current type of union for couples. Table 8.3 provides insight into the mean ages at marriage. As follows from the total number of respondents at this question, the majority of the second generation lives with a married partner, whereas around a third of the comparison group couples lives in an unmarried union. Overall, second-generation Turkish young adults marry the youngest, at the average age of 21.3, followed by second-generation Moroccans and young adults of the comparison group (on average, 22.5 and 27.7 years old, respectively). Again, we find that women of all groups marry at a younger age than do their male counterparts. We find about a two-year age difference for second-generation Turks and comparison group respondents. At four years, the age difference between men and women is the largest for the Moroccan second generation.

When we compare ages at marriage with those at cohabitation (see Table 8.2), we find that, for the second generation, they are almost the same. In general, these young adults get married and then start living with their partners. The only exception is found among second-generation Moroccan men: we find that the average age at marriage is six months plus the age at which they began living with their partner. This indicates a period of unmarried cohabitation among this group. According to the averages ages, the comparison group clearly delays marriage: they start living with their partners around 25 and got married to their

Table 8.3 *Mean age at marriage to current partner, by ethnic group and sex*

	Second generation						Comparison group		
	Turks			Moroccans					
	Men	Women	Total	Men	Women	Total	Men	Women	Total
Mean age at marriage	22.5	20.5	21.3	25.2	21.3	22.5	28.7	26.9	27.7
Standard deviation	3.0	3.3	3.3	2.8	3.1	3.5	3.4	3.6	3.6
N	80	113	193	28	65	93	33	42	75

current partners about 2.5 years later. Men from the comparison group seem to postpone marriage even more than do women from this group in the TIES survey.

8.4 Meeting places and family influence

Where did those with current partners meet this person? Table 8.4 gives an overview of this information according to group of origin. It is clear that a fifth of the second-generation young adults met their current partner during a vacation in their parents' country of origin. For second-generation Turks, the second most common place to meet their partner was at a family event; the third was at school. Meanwhile, for second-generation Moroccans, family events are the third most common meeting place and meeting through friends ranks second. One-fifth of the comparison group met their partners at school, another fifth did so through friends, and another fifth, while going out. The workplace proved to be another important meeting place for young adults of the comparison group.

The decision to get married is made by the couple themselves, though it may also involve family influences. When asked about influences by their own family or their spouse's family to get married, the second generation clearly reports more pressure than the comparison group (Table 8.5). A third of the second-generation respondents say their family or their in-laws encouraged them to get married. At the same time, their own family or their spouse's family also put pressure

Table 8.4 *Place of meeting current partner, by ethnic group*

	Second generation		Comparison group
	Turks	Moroccans	
At school	13.3	7.9	18.7
At work	7.2	7.9	14.5
Through friends	9.6	18.4	18.7
At a sports club	1.2	5.3	5.7
Going out	1.2	5.3	18.9
At a family reunion/festivity	15.7	10.5	1.3
Introduction through parents	7.2	2.6	0.0
On vacation in parents' country of origin	22.9	21.1	1.3
On vacation elsewhere	7.2	2.6	3.2
Through network of friends	2.4	2.6	0.4
In the neighborhood	3.6	2.6	3.2
In a public place	2.4	5.3	1.3
Other	6.0	7.9	12.8
Total	100.0	100.0	100.0
N	223	114	220

UNION AND FAMILY FORMATION

Table 8.5 *Family influences on decision-making regarding marriage, by ethnic group*

	Second generation		Comparison group
	Turks	Moroccans	
Pressure to get married by own family/in-laws			
Yes	34.7	32.3	13.9
No	65.3	67.7	86.1
Total	100.0	100.0	100.0
N	195	96	76
Pressure to abstain from marriage by own family/in-laws			
Yes	15.3	6.5	2.9
No	84.7	93.5	97.1
Total	100.0	100.0	100.0
N	195	96	76

on the second generation to abstain from marriage, especially among Turkish young adults. Although it is often assumed that young adults in the comparison group make independent decisions without much involvement of their families, 14 per cent of the respondents of this group said their family encouraged them to get married. Just a few of these young adults felt that their family pressured them to refrain from getting married to their current partner.

A small number of respondents (N = 70) also provided information about how the decision to get married was made (not in table). The majority among all groups, including 100 per cent of the second-generation Moroccans, said they, themselves, wanted to get married. Some 15 per cent of the second-generation Turkish and 6 per cent of the comparison group respondents said they did not want to get married, but agreed to it eventually. These figures suggest that most pressure is put on the Turkish second generation, either through support of or disagreement with the marriage.

8.5 Partner choice: partner characteristics

The ethnic origin of the second generation's current partners generally match findings on a couple's place of meeting. Overall, we find that slightly more than two-thirds of all respondents has a first-generation partner from their own group (last column of Table 8.6). However, there are clear differences when we distinguish between the age groups. Of the Turkish respondents in the oldest age groups, 81 per cent has a first-generation partner, whereas the number comprises 58 per cent for the youngest age groups. Changes are even more remarkable for the Moroccan second generation: 88 per cent of the oldest group has a first-generation partner compared to a third of the youngest age group.

Table 8.6 *Origin of partner, by ethnic group and age group*

	Second generation						Comparison group		
	Turks			Moroccan					
Partner's origin	18-24	25-29	30+	18-24	25-29	30+	18-24	25-29	30+
Dutch origin	0.0	2.4	4.8	11.1	0.0	0.0	79.4	80.1	69.8
Second generation own group: one foreign-born parent	5.3	0.0	0.0	11.1	0.0	0.0	0.0	0.0	0.0
Second generation own group: two foreign-born parents	26.3	26.8	9.5	33.3	20.0	12.5	0.0	0.0	0.0
Second generation: born elsewhere	10.5	0.0	4.8	11.1	5.0	0.0	9.5	7.0	12.3
First generation own group: one foreign-born parent	0.0	0.0	0.0	0.0	5.0	0.0	0.0	0.0	0.0
First generation own group: two foreign-born parents	57.9	68.3	81.0	33.0	65.0	87.5	0.0	0.6	0.0
First generation: born elsewhere	0.0	2.4	0.0	0.0	5.0	0.0	11.1	12.3	17.9
Total	100.0	100.0	100.0	100.0	100.0	100.0	100.0	100.0	100.0
N	47	113	58	27	56	30	30	74	113

From their ages at migration, it is obvious that a quarter of first-generation partners came to the Netherlands before the age of fifteen. Thus, the majority of these first-generation partners were not raised in the Netherlands.

The decreasing percentage of first-generation partners across the cohorts is accompanied by a clear increase in the percentages of respondents who have a second-generation partner. Around 10 per cent of those aged 30 or above has a second-generation partner, whereas for those between eighteen and 24 years, the number rises to 31 per cent for the Turkish second generation and 44 per cent for the Moroccan second generation. The level of inter-partnering with a person of Dutch origin is also found to be extremely low among the second generation. All in all, this seems to indicate an increasing preference to choose a partner from the second generation among the youngest cohorts. At the same time, one must be aware that the sharp increase in the number of second-generation youth in the Netherlands in recent years also offers more options to choose a second-generation partner than would have been available to the oldest respondents in the TIES survey. Finally, we should be cautious with interpreting these findings and trends, as the number of respondents in each of the age groups is rather limited.

Concerning the ethnic origin of partners of the comparison group, we find rather stable patterns across the age cohorts. The majority of the respondents (three-quarters) has a partner who is of Dutch origin. Others have partners of first or second generations, but none of them is of Turkish or Moroccan origin. These patterns are found to be stable among different age groups.

In line with findings on the second-generation partners' country of origin, results show that a majority of the partners holds the nationality of the country of origin: 78 per cent of the partners of the Turkish second generation and 68 per cent of the partners of the Moroccan second generation (not in table). Additionally, we find that a third of the Turkish second generation and 46 per cent of the Moroccan second generation report that their partners have dual nationality: Dutch and Turkish or Dutch and Moroccan.

The survey also assessed the educational level of the partner. Compared with the other groups, partners of the second-generation Turkish respondents have the lowest educational level and those of the comparison group, the highest; second-generation Moroccans take an intermediate position (not in table). Each of the groups differs significantly from one another. Research has shown that people nowadays often have a partner with the same educational background. We therefore included the educational level of both partners in the analyses. We assessed the current level for those respondents who were receiving education and the final level for those who left the educational system. Those respondents who had the same educational level as their partners were labelled homogamous couples. Table 8.7 shows that the Turkish second generation has the lowest level of educational homogamy; a fifth of the partners in these unions has the same educational level. This percentage is clearly higher for the Moroccan second generation and the highest for the comparison group respondents, of whom a third and two-fifths, respectively, are in an educationally homogamous union. However, the level of educational homogamy is not significantly different between the Moroccan second generation and Dutch. We did not find any significant differences in the level of educational homogamy between age groups.

The second generation was also asked about whether their partners were related by blood to their own families. Table 8.8 gives the percentages of partners who were related to their spouses by blood. The majority of the second generation, 81 per cent of the Turks and 88 per cent of

Table 8.7 *Couples with same educational level, by ethnic group*

	Second generation		
	Turks	Moroccans	Comparison group
No	80.5	71.1	58.7
Yes	19.5	28.9	41.3
Total	100.0	100.0	100.0
N	223	114	220

Table 8.8 *Family links between partners, by ethnic group*

	Second generation	
	Turks	Moroccans
Cousins	8.3	6.3
Other family relationship	11.1	6.3
No family	80.6	87.5
Total	100.0	100.0
N	223	114

the Moroccans, report that their partners were non-family members. The Turkish second generation is more likely than the Moroccan to be in a union where partners were cousins or of some other blood relation. Nevertheless, the differences between the second-generation groups are not significant.

Finally, we looked at the current situations of partners of the second generation and the comparison group. Table 8.9 gives an overview of their current daily activities. For all three groups, we find that women overall report having partners who have a job or their own business. The percentage with a paid job is highest among the comparison group and lowest for the partners of second-generation Turkish men. The partners of the second-generation Turkish women have the highest levels of entrepreneurship. A substantial number of second-generation Moroccan women (17 per cent) report that their partners are unemployed and looking for a job.

Table 8.9 *Current situation of the partner, by ethnic group and sex of the respondent*

	Second generation				Comparison group	
	Turks		Moroccan			
	Men	Women	Men	Women	Men	Women
Has one or more paid jobs	32.4	67.4	54.5	70.8	70.6	79.6
Has own business	0.0	15.2	0.0	4.2	4.4	5.1
Works freelance	0.0	4.3	0.0	0.0	5.6	4.7
Has a job and is in school	5.4	4.3	9.1	4.2	2.8	6.6
Has internship related to education	2.7	0.0	0.0	0.0	1.2	1.8
Has unpaid work	2.7	0.0	0.0	0.0	0.0	0.0
Unemployed though not seeking a job	2.7	2.2	0.0	0.0	0.0	0.0
Unemployed and seeking a job	2.7	4.3	0.0	16.7	0.0	1.5
Takes care of the children	40.5	0.0	27.3	0.0	5.2	0.0
Is unable to work	0.0	0.0	0.0	0.0	0.4	0.4
Is a student	5.4	0.0	9.1	4.2	9.1	0.4
Don't know	5.4	2.2	0.0	0.0	0.8	0.0
Total	100.0	100.0	100.0	100.0	100.0	100.0
N	94	129	38	76	105	115

When looking at the activities that men report of their partners, we find that having a paid job and looking after children are the most common activities among all groups. However, the comparison group's labour force participation among women is much higher than that among the second generation. Whereas 71 per cent of the female partners of the comparison group are reported as having a paid job, this is the case for only 55 per cent among second-generation Moroccans and 32 per cent among second-generation Turks. Substantial shares, between 27 and 41 per cent, of the partners of second-generation men are reported to take care of the children.

Although being a student is the activity of female partners mentioned third most frequently, the percentage of male partners who are in education is slight. Partners seem to start living together only once they are no longer studying. The differences between men and women are no doubt related to the fact that the men are, on average, older (and thus less likely to still be in education) than women, though it may also indicate that having a more stable job position is linked to cohabiting more so for men than for women.

8.6 Family formation

An important decision in a young adult's life is the choice of whether and when to have children. The analyses show that the majority of young adults in the TIES survey do not have children yet (Table 8.10). Second-generation Turks are most likely to have children, while comparison group members are the least likely. Taking the somewhat younger age structure of the Moroccan respondents into account shows that second-generation Moroccans do have children more often than the comparison group. Almost a quarter of the Turkish second generation has at least one child and 13 per cent has a second child already. These findings are an indication that this group starts family formation earlier and generally will have more children than the comparison group.

The second part of Table 8.10 shows the mean ages at birth of the first child for men and for women. Second-generation Turkish women are the youngest to have their first child, and women from the comparison group are the oldest. One must bear in mind that the mean ages at first birth for the whole group will be higher. Those who already have children are likely to prove a select group: by far, the majority of young adults in the TIES survey did not have children.

Table 8.10 *Current number of children and mean age at birth of first child, by ethnic group*

	Second generation		Comparison group
	Turks	Moroccans	
Number of children			
0	62.6	78.9	80.1
1	22.4	12.0	13.8
2	12.6	5.1	5.3
3	2.3	3.4	0.9
4	0.0	0.0	0.0
5	0.0	0.6	0.0
Total	100.0	100.0	100.0
N	500	493	512
Mean age at birth of first child			
Men	24.4	27.1	29.4
Standard deviation	3.0	3.4	3.6
N	58	16	29
Women	22.4	22.8	27.0
Standard deviation	3.4	3.9	4.5
N	99	60	60

8.7 Task division

Couples living together must decide who will do the household chores, who will take care of the children and who will participate in the labour force. Table 8.11 gives an overview of who mainly takes care of certain tasks, according to group of origin. The results show that among the second generation, around 40 per cent of household tasks are performed by the woman. The majority of the second-generation Moroccans and the comparison group say household chores are shared among family members. This does not imply that the sharing is equal. Respondents could also choose to answer that both partners shared this task equally, though none did so on any of the task division items.

For the second generation, we find that cooking is typically a responsibility of the woman; couples in the comparison group mainly share this task. Respondents were also asked who takes care of finances. For each of the groups, we find that larger shares of men than women take up this task. Although at least a third of the couples do share the task, the Moroccan couples and comparison group couples, in particular, report that family members take up this task together. Earning an income is the joint responsibility for the majority of Moroccan (71 per cent) and comparison group couples (79 per cent). Almost half of the Turkish respondents state that it is the man who primarily takes care of this.

Finally, those respondents who were parents were asked about who primarily takes care of the children. Among the second generation, it is

Table 8.11 *Division of tasks in the household, by ethnic group*

	Second generation		Comparison group
	Turks	Moroccans	
Household chores			
Man	26.6	13.5	16.2
Woman	39.2	37.8	22.8
Family members together	34.2	48.6	60.9
Total	100.0	100.0	100.0
N	213	107	208
Cooking			
Man	38.0	25.0	31.5
Woman	44.3	50.0	22.0
Family members together	17.7	25.0	46.5
Total	100.0	100.0	100.0
N	213	105	192
Finances and administration			
Man	36.8	31.0	31.3
Woman	27.9	27.6	21.8
Family members together	35.3	41.4	46.8
Total	100.0	100.0	100.0
N	182	90	190
Earning income			
Man	46.6	21.4	14.1
Woman	5.2	7.1	6.4
Family members together	48.3	71.4	79.5
Total	100.0	100.0	100.0
N	152	85	186
Taking care of children			
Man	31.5	15.0	21.7
Woman	40.7	55.0	35.5
Family members together	27.8	30.0	43.3
Total	100.0	100.0	100.0
N	143	63	76

mainly the woman, although around one-third of the second-generation couples shares in the childcare. Though couples of the comparison group are more likely to care for children together, still one-third indicates that it is primarily the woman taking up this task.

As already mentioned, the fact that many tasks are shared among household members does not imply equal sharing. In addition, household chores and taking care of children cover a range of activities. It could very well be that the division of specific tasks follows clear gender lines.

When respondents were asked about whether they were happy with the current household division of tasks, the overwhelming majority indicated that they were (Table 8.12). In general, men were happier with the arrangement than the women were, though sex differences are neg-

Table 8.12 Whether respondents are happy with division of tasks between household partners, by ethnic group and sex

	Second generation		Comparison group
	Turks	Moroccans	
Men			
Yes	97.2	92.3	95.6
No	2.8	7.7	4.4
Total	100.0	100.0	100.0
N	94	38	105
Women			
Yes	82.6	80.0	95.3
No	17.4	20.0	4.7
Total	100.0	100.0	100.0
N	129	76	115

ligible for the comparison group. A substantial share, however, of the Turkish and Moroccan second-generation women (17 and 20 per cent, respectively) were not happy with the way tasks were divided between themselves and their partners. Unfortunately, we do not have information on what they would like to change.

Finally, respondents who have children were asked about whether they themselves or their partner held a paid job before having their first child. Table 8.13 shows that the majority of men had a paid job before the birth of their first child. Labour force participation by Moroccan men is the lowest and that by men of the comparison group, the highest. When asked about the labour force participation by their partners before they had children, one-third of the second-generation men reported their partners having a job. Compared to the self-reported participation of the second-generation women in the TIES survey, this is rather low. It may very well be related to the fact that a substantial share of the partners of the second-generation men in the study are of the first generation (see paragraph on partner characteristics). Two-thirds of the second-generation women in the study say they had a job before giving birth. Women of the comparison group in our survey participate at a somewhat higher rate; 90 per cent had a job.

The last table of this chapter (Table 8.14) shows the change in labour force participation for second-generation men and women after having their first child. Second-generation men are mainly found to keep to the same working hours as they had before. Substantial shares of second-generation men also increase their working hours; 17 per cent of the Turks and 10 per cent of the Moroccans work more hours, compared with only 5 per cent of the men of the comparison group. A reverse pattern is found among women. A minority does not change working hours. Second-generation Turkish women are most likely to

Table 8.13 *Labour force participation of men and women before birth of first child, by ethnic group*

		Second generation		Comparison group
		Turks	Moroccans	
Male respondents themselves	Yes	88.5	75.0	97.7
	No	11.5	25.0	2.3
	Total	100.0	100.0	100.0
	N	70	33	33
Female partners according to male respondent	Yes	36.0	33.3	85.3
	No	56.0	66.7	14.7
	Total	100.0	100.0	100.0
	N	65	18	30
Female respondents themselves	Yes	64.1	68.0	90.2
	No	35.9	32.0	9.8
	Total	100.0	100.0	100.0
	N	107	74	64
Male partners according to female respondents	Yes	78.8	82.4	92.9
	No	18.2	11.8	6.2
	Total	100.0	100.0	100.0
	N	92	53	50

Table 8.14 *Change in labour force participation after childbirth, by ethnic group and sex*

	Second generation				Comparison group	
	Turks		Moroccans			
	Men	Women	Men	Women	Men	Women
More hours	16.7	0.0	10.0	5.9	4.7	0.0
Fewer hours	0.0	33.3	20.0	35.3	37.6	59.7
Stopped working	0.0	33.3	0.0	35.3	0.0	13.2
No change	83.3	33.3	70.0	23.5	57.6	27.1
Total	100.0	100.0	100.0	100.0	100.0	100.0
N	60	71	24	51	31	55

keep their previous working hours, and second-generation Moroccan women are least likely. Around a third of the second-generation women quit the labour market, and another third reduces the number of hours worked. Women of the comparison group most often choose to reduce the number of hours. Only a minority of women of the comparison group, at 13 per cent, stopped their paid job when they had their first child.

8.8 Conclusions

This chapter provided some impressions on union and family formation among the second generation and the comparison group. We find that the second generation is more likely to have a married partner, whereas the comparison group lives with a partner in an unmarried union. When it comes to partner choice, we also find clear changes between the different age cohorts of the second generation. The youngest age groups, for example, have a second-generation partner more often than do the oldest age group, whose partners are mostly of the first generation.

Furthermore, it is often assumed that Turks and Moroccans marry a partner who is related by blood to their own family. According to the TIES data, this is still rather common among the Turkish second generation, one in five of whom has a spouse they share pre-marital family links with. Marrying a family member seems to be less common among the Moroccan second generation.

With respect to childbearing, we find that Turks start family formation at a younger age than do Moroccans or the comparison group. More than a third of the Turkish second generation in our sample already had at least one child, as compared with about 20 per cent among the Moroccan second generation and the comparison group.

When it comes to task division in the household, we find that many tasks are shared between partners. Given the limited labour force participation of Turkish and Moroccan women from the first generation, it is interesting to find that earning an income is a joint task for most of the TIES respondents. Again, Turks seem to follow the male-as-breadwinner model more often than the other two groups do. The Moroccan second generation also seems to behave rather similarly to the Dutch.

Overall, we can conclude that the union and family formation processes of the Turkish second generation still follow more traditional patterns than is the case for their Moroccan counterparts. When it comes to different aspects of union and family formation, the Moroccan second generation finds themselves in an intermediate position, between Turks and the comparison group.

References

Garssen, J. & H. Nicolaas (2006), 'Recente trends in de vruchtbaarheid van niet-westerse allochtone vrouwen', *Bevolkingstrends* 1: 15-31.
Garssen, J. & M. Wageveld (2007), 'Demografie' in J. Dagevos & M. Gijsberts (eds.), *Jaarrapport integratie 2007*, 29-46. The Hague: Sociaal Cultureel Plan Bureau.
Huis, M. Van (2007), 'Partnerkeuze van allochtonen', *Bevolkingstrends* 4: 25-31.

Immigration and Naturalization Service (2006), *The civic integration examination abroad.* March 2006. The Hague: IND.

Immigration and Naturalization Service (2007), *Residence in the Netherlands.* December 2007. The Hague: IND.

Immigration and Naturalization Service (2008), *Costs for staying in the Netherlands fact sheet.* February 2008. The Hague: IND.

Valk, H.A.G. De, I. Esveldt, K. Henkens & A.C. Liefbroer (2001), *Oude en nieuwe allochtonen in Nederland: Een demografisch profiel* (WRR working document W123). The Hague: Wetenschappelijke Raad voor het Regeringsbeleid.

9 Conclusions and implications[1]

Maurice Crul, George Groenewold and Liesbeth Heering

The second generation of Turkish and Moroccan descent in the Netherlands is currently coming of age, and the older cohorts have already made the transition from education to the labour market. This means that, for the first time, we can make a genuine assessment of the position of second generations in Dutch society. The TIES project aims to engage in such an assessment by examining a variety of topics. Its foremost interest lies in aspects of *structural* integration: analysing access to and participation in domains such as education and the labour market. Additionally, the survey includes topics relevant to *social* integration, such as social relationships, family formation and partner choice, religion and identity. The TIES survey was directed at three different groups of respondents in the two major cities of Amsterdam and Rotterdam: the Dutch-born direct descendents of immigrants from Turkey, the Dutch-born direct descendents of immigrants from Morocco and a comparison group with no migration background at the parent level. The selected age group was that of eighteen to 35 year olds.

The term 'comparison group' was used throughout this report rather than 'native Dutch' or simply 'Dutch'. The most important reason for this is the fact that the second generations included in the TIES study are – by definition – also native-born, and many thus have the nationality of their country of birth.

In the *domains of education* and *the labour market,* the dominant public image of the second generations oscillates between feelings of concern and feelings of optimism. It is the classic half-full or half-empty glass dilemma. The main findings indicate that the dilemma corresponds with reality: a considerable part of the second generation is doing very well, while others lag behind. Perhaps the most striking outcome is the degree of polarisation *within* the second-generation groups.

Short educational careers have proven to be an important indicator of staying behind. Among those who completed their education, about 50 per cent did not obtain the entrance qualification (*startkwalificatie*) that is defined as the minimum level of completed education required to successfully enter the labour market. Children without such entrance qualifications are officially labelled 'at-risk' youth, and they make up approximately a quarter of the entire sample. As can be expected, the at-risk group also figures prominently among the long-term unemployed, and they tend to remain dependent on financial support from the government. Also overrepresented in this group are married women, whose principal activity is to raise their children. This group is largest among second-generation Turkish women.

Those who are doing well are usually still enrolled in educational programmes. This is most clearly visible among the second-generation Moroccans who are pursuing careers in higher education or have just made the transition from higher education to work. Half of the members of this group did not move straight through the school system, but took the long route, starting at lower secondary vocational education or general secondary education and continuing through middle vocational education to finally end up in tertiary education (mostly higher vocational education). Pursuing this long route requires persistence and ambition, as exemplified by women who finished higher education and found they could convert their educational success into favourable labour market positions. These women postpone getting married and having children. Average marriage ages among Turkish and Moroccan second-generation women are rising primarily because of this phenomenon.

A similar picture emerges when we look at labour market positions. While the great majority of second-generation Turks have already completed their transition to the labour market, this applies to only half of the Moroccan second-generation group. Furthermore, we see both positive and negative outcomes on the labour market; unemployment is relatively high in both groups. Ten per cent of the second-generation Turks is unemployed and actively seeking work; for second-generation Moroccans, the figure is 8 per cent. This is four to five times higher than the figures for the comparison group. Also, the educational position of the comparison group is much better: only 10 per cent does not have an entrance qualification (i.e. they leave school prematurely).

Second-generation Turks and Moroccans predominantly occupy lower and secondary job positions. This offers a stark contrast with the comparison group, more than 50 per cent of whom works in highly skilled and scientific jobs. In the other two groups, this applies to a mere 20 per cent.

The Moroccan second-generation group would seem to occupy the worst position in the labour market. Here, more people hold elementary jobs. Though at the same time, in this group, the younger cohorts in our study are overrepresented, and – as stated above – they remain enrolled in education longer than second-generation Turks. Thus, the comparison may change drastically once those in higher education have completed their education and join the labour market.

In the second-generation groups, women on the labour market do slightly better than men. Women are more likely to work in service sectors such as health care, social work and education, all of which are currently in desperate need of employees. Moreover, and particularly in the major cities, employers are especially wont to recruit employees from different cultural and linguistic backgrounds in order to meet the ever-increasing demand for social and health care needs among first-generation immigrants.

A comparison of income levels shows a clear improvement for the Turkish second generation over their Moroccan counterparts. Again, this can partly be explained by the fact that more second-generation Moroccans are still enrolled in education, living off study grants and/or small part-time jobs. The moment more highly educated Moroccans enter the labour market, the difference between the Turkish and Moroccan second generation may disappear, or even become inverted. Final conclusions can only be drawn after the necessary follow-up research into this issue has been completed.

More favourable income situations lead to a larger proportion of second-generation Turks becoming homeowners. This holds true for one-third of those Turkish respondents who live outside their parents' households. This is a remarkable finding, considering the fact that Amsterdam and Rotterdam have such a large public housing sector. Second-generation Turkish homeowners live in single-family dwellings more often than the comparison group, and almost half of them even own fairly new homes (built less than 25 years ago).

In line with the trend towards leaving school earlier, second-generation Turks also marry and have children at younger ages than do second-generation Moroccans. More than half of the second-generation Turkish women who left their parents' household did so because they got married. By contrast, members from the largest group among second-generation Moroccan women who live separately from their parents did so in order to undertake studies in higher education or to live on their own.

With regard to partner choice and family formation, the Turkish second generation seems most oriented towards its own group and their parents' country of origin. Members of this group often find their partners while on family holidays in Turkey or at community events. In about half of the marriages, Turkish parents exerted some degree of positive or negative pressure. One in five partners is a blood relative. In terms of gender roles, the Turkish second-generation group seems to be most traditional. Some 41 per cent of second-generation Turkish wives have not entered the labour market and take care of the children, while, among the comparison group, the share of female working partners is twice as high. Interestingly, the majority of Moroccan second-generation men also have a working partner. Most second-generation respondents married someone from their own ethnic background. The most notable trend here is that our respondents increasingly seem to opt for partners who, like themselves, are second-generation. Still, the majority of partners who have so far been selected are immigrants.

With regard to identities and identification, the study confirms the expectation that people may have strong feelings of belonging at simultaneously different levels. For most respondents, feelings of being 'Moroccan' or 'Turkish' blend well with a local and/or a national identity. The same is found for the combination of Muslim identity with local and national belonging. The second generation does not seem to see these identities as being mutually exclusive – inasmuch as the general societal discourse on the topic seems to suggest differently. Possibly as the result of being less contested, local identity is particularly strong, especially when compared with national identity. Two-thirds of the second-generation respondents express that they experience a strong or very strong identity as *'Amsterdammers'* or *'Rotterdammers'*. Furthermore, respondents who still live with their parents also express a strong neighbourhood attachment.

Religion plays a major role in the lives of second-generation Turks and Moroccans. This is particularly true for the latter group, among which almost half the respondents state that religion is of major importance to them. This does not necessarily mean that religious *practices* play an equally important role: the majority sees religion predominantly as a private matter and never or only rarely do they visit a mosque. A large proportion of the second generation never prays at all. Those who do pray daily or weekly and are active in other religious practices nevertheless form a considerable minority, being about a quarter of the respondents from Turkish and Moroccan backgrounds.

Another question is whether religious identity translates into political viewpoints or attitudes concerning gender roles. Although the second generation differs from the comparison group on a number of societal issues, the differences found are not very large. For instance, as regards gender roles, very few second-generation respondents perceive education to be more important for boys than it is for girls. Only a small minority feels that women should not have jobs if they have young children (a stance not uncommon among conservatives in the majority society, either). Less than 10 per cent says they would find it a problem if they had a female superior at work. And only a small minority says they want Islam to play a more political role in society.

Often ignored, however, has been the group for which religion plays *no role at all*, and this is where the main difference is found between the two second-generation groups and the comparison group. Only one in ten second-generation respondents states that they have no religion at all, while more than eight out of ten respondents in the comparison group claim not to belong to any religious denomination. This difference could pose a major challenge for cross-group relations in the major cities. In Amsterdam, however, the comparison group, which is mostly secular, is quite positive about religious diversity: almost two-thirds agree that having different religions coexisting in the city is a good thing. Meanwhile in Rotterdam, this opinion is shared only by 39 per cent. The Rotterdam comparison group proves to be much more negative in other statements related to the multicultural society; they are also less willing to admit that racism and discrimination occur on the labour market for people of Turkish or Moroccan descent. The survey thus seems to support the widespread stereotype that Amsterdam is a more tolerant place than Rotterdam. Nevertheless, this does not mean that the second-generation group members would feel very comfortable in Amsterdam. It is particularly the second-generation Moroccans who think that the city's climate has become less friendly over the past few years.

9.1 Study implications

The most disturbing result for policymakers must be the fact that one-quarter of the second-generation respondents in the survey has no proper entrance qualification to the labour market. Their position in society is highly vulnerable and socially insecure. They run high risks of remaining at the bottom of the hourglass economies of the major cities, hardly rising above the socio-economic status of their immigrant parents. They will most probably continue to live in the same type of neighbourhoods in which they grew up, and these neighbourhoods will have become more segregated over time. Their children will visit schools that are more likely to be qualified by school inspectors as the 'worst-performing schools'. Moreover, the majority of this group is likely to marry a partner from their parents' country of origin, who will likely be generally ill-prepared for the Dutch labour market. In sum, the future for one-quarter of the second-generation population does not look promising. Because of unstable job situations, members of this group will most probably become or remain dependent on social housing, if not welfare, and their children will grow up at or around the poverty level.

The relatively large proportion of at-risk respondents among the second generation contrasts strongly with the comparison group. Here, the vast majority is highly educated, and often both partners have paid jobs. This obviously also leads to considerable differences in income, causing a potential 'ethnic split' in society in which we may witness the rise of a group of poor people of primarily immigrant background versus the rise of predominantly 'white' upper and middle classes.

The key to counteracting this undesirable development is education. Too many children of immigrant parents leave school prematurely. The educational institutions are not equipped to keep these children aboard. As the TIES survey shows, more than half of the at-risk youth were originally enrolled in lower general secondary education (vmbo-t) or higher levels. They should therefore, in theory, be able to finish a two-year middle vocational education track based on their proven abilities in secondary school. The fact that a large group does not succeed in doing so suggests considerable institutional problems in middle vocational education in the Dutch school system.

The development of a middle class of migrant backgrounds (be they first-, second- or third-generation) will prove crucial for cities in countering possible ethnic polarisation. The TIES findings reported here give reason for optimism. Almost one-third of the second generation is either enrolled in higher education or has already finished their studies. Members of this group will be the future agents of upward social mobility in their communities. They will find high-level jobs. They will become entrepreneurs and company owners. They will be active as representatives of immigrant or religious organisations. They will marry at a later age, and their partners will often also be well-educated and working, thus increasing the number of double incomes. They will often move out of their childhood neighbourhoods or occupy apartments in the better parts of their old neighbourhoods. The children of these parents will subsequently grow up in financially steady, middle-class families and enjoy favourable prospects for the future. Moreover, because of their studies and work, they are also likely to develop more contacts outside their own ethnic community circles.

It is important to note that among this successful second-generation group, many have followed the so-called long route through education, starting in lower vocational education to finally arrive in higher education. This educational itinerary takes up to three years longer than the direct route. Although it is significant that this route is available – a road which has traditionally been a main mobility path for Dutch working-class children as well – many pupils nevertheless drop out in this phase. The fact that many successful students in higher education were originally advised to enter lower vocational education also raises questions about the validity and the application mechanisms of that recommendation process.

The transition to the labour market of the at-risk group in our survey alerts us to two important insights. On the one hand, the labour market does not simply work as a return on the educational investment. Some respondents with low educational achievements have obtained regular

CONCLUSIONS AND IMPLICATIONS 167

jobs on the labour market or even made it into skilled professions. Precisely how this has happened should be the subject of further analyses, but it shows the *in*clusive effect of the labour market. On the other hand, there are obviously additional *ex*clusive effects, such as discrimination, to which the at-risk group is most vulnerable.

With regard to polarisation *within* the second-generation groups – between a growing successful middle class and a stabilising at-risk group – the two crucial questions for the future will be whether the middle-class second-generation groups can be kept in the cities, and whether it is possible to have these groups act as a sort of cement between the at-risk group and the wider society. The use of their social and cultural capital may well be a decisive factor in building a socially cohesive urban society.

What can be said about the willingness expressed by second-generation youth to be part of Dutch society? Our findings show that almost half of the second generation agrees or totally agrees with the statement that migrants and their children should live their lives outside the home according to Dutch norms and values *as much as possible*. It should be kept in mind that a large group is making a strong statement here. At the same time, however, many of them also feel that migrants and their children should live their lives outside the home according to *Turkish or Moroccan* norms as much as possible. Although not measured by the survey, these respondents may distinguish between public behaviour towards their own group members (for example, at a Turkish wedding) and public behaviour towards Dutch people. Also, one in five second-generation youngsters *disagrees* with the statement that migrants and their children should live their lives outside the home according to Dutch norms and values. Instead, they feel that Turkish or Moroccan migrants and their children should live their lives outside the home according to Turkish or Moroccan norms and values. This position, of course, severely limits their interaction with other ethnic groups.

Equally important, however, is the attitude of the majority society. Here, differences in the attitudes expressed among the comparison groups in Rotterdam and in Amsterdam towards multicultural society and immigrants suggest differences in city contexts.

We should not look just at the relationship between the second-generation groups and what is frequently referred to as the 'native Dutch'. The major cities are becoming increasingly heterogeneous and, especially in the younger cohorts, the 'native Dutch' are becoming as much an ethnic minority group as the others. Thus, part of the climate in which the second-generation Turks and Moroccans grow up in Rotterdam and in Amsterdam is also defined by their relationship with the large communities originating from Indonesia, Surinam, the Antilles and other nations. Moreover, as a result of interaction and intermarriage, people with mixed ethnic backgrounds are becoming more and more visible in urban life. Of the comparison group in our survey, one-quarter of the respondents has a partner with a 'non-Dutch' background.

As a final point, TIES also shows that it is members of the comparison group who are in fact newcomers to the city. Contrary to what was seen in the second-generation groups, a majority was not born and/or raised in Amsterdam or in Rotterdam. Thus, it is mostly this group who must adapt to the new city environment. Given the fact that many of these individuals will also leave the city again at some point in time, either for professional or family reasons, they might be called the 'sojourners' of Amsterdam and Rotterdam.

Note

1   A Dutch translation of this chapter can be found at the end of this volume.

Appendix: Sample design, TIES survey implementation and evaluation

George Groenewold

1.1 Sample design

The survey in the Netherlands focussed on generating statistically representative data on second-generation Turks and Moroccans in the main urban areas of concentration of these two groups: Amsterdam and Rotterdam. The level of statistical representativeness is the combined population of both cities, including the second generation of both ethnic groups and a comparison group of similar persons with both parents born in the Netherlands. Below, the latter is addressed in more detail. Data collection and processing were subcontracted to the professional survey company Bureau Veldkamp in Amsterdam.

The *minimum effective sample size* was set at 1,500 persons, with 750 in each city and 250 persons of each ethnic group within each city. Thus, city of residence and ethnic group membership were explicit stratification variables.

In the case of the Netherlands, a sampling frame of members of the aforementioned groups is readily available in the form of a municipal population register (GBA). This register contains basic information on all persons who are legal residents in the municipality. The *de jure* population is recorded, and this differs to some extent from the *de facto* population because of the presence of unrecorded immigrants originating from other cities in the country or from abroad and because of the absence of residents who failed to inform the municipal authorities about their move away from the city. However, because most administrative dealings with the municipal or central government require citizens to present a 'proof of legal residence', it is in the interests of most residents to ensure that their registration is properly done and up-to-date. Several pieces of information are recorded in the population register, such as date of birth, sex, country of birth, country of birth of father, country of birth of mother, full address, nationality and marital status. This makes the register an obvious choice for sampling addresses of members of ethnic groups (BPR 2006).

To determine the *gross sample size*, studies on response behaviour in the Netherlands were examined. These show that response rates to general social science surveys have been declining in the past decades but also that marked improvements have occurred since the mid-1990s as a result of applying new fieldwork strategies and instruments (De Heer & De Leeuw 1999; Stoop 2005). For instance, the most recent European Social Science Survey (2004) conducted in the Netherlands resulted in a 64.3 per cent response rate, similar to rates in Belgium (61.2 per cent), Austria (62.4 per cent) and Sweden (64.4 per cent), and considerably higher than in France (43.6 per cent), Switzerland (48.6 per cent), Germany (51.0 per cent) and Spain (54.9 per cent). Various studies show that place of residence and not ethnic affiliation is the most important predictor for response rates. For instance, Schmeets and Van der Bie (2005) show that response rates in the large cities are considerably lower than elsewhere in the Netherlands and that response rates among first-generation and second-generation descendants of non-western immigrants are below average. They demonstrate that differences between the response rates of ethnic groups within the large cities are far less striking than is generally assumed. In fact, they show that the observed ethnic differences in response rates in the country are mainly due to place of residence and not so much to ethnic origin. This is because most ethnic minority groups live in the largest cities where the response rates are the lowest, including those of people of Dutch descent. The 2004 Permanent Living Conditions Survey (POLS) shows that the response rate of second-generation descendants of non-western immigrants in Amsterdam was 33 per cent, while the rate of those of Dutch descent was not much higher, being 41 per cent. Figures for Rotterdam were 52 and 53 per cent, respectively. Within the group of descendants of non-western immigrants, figures for second-generation Turks and Moroccans appear to be below average. Furthermore, recent research (Crok et al. 2004; Gemeente Amsterdam 2006) on the integration of ethnic minorities in Amsterdam shows that, among residents of non-western origin, members of the Moroccan and Turkish ethnic groups show the least progress in terms of indicators of socioeconomic, cultural and political integration, including spatial segregation. This may further contribute to lower than expected response rates among members of these groups. Therefore, it was decided to increase the minimum effective sample sizes in both cities by a factor of four, leading to a gross sample size of 6,271. This includes a supplementary sample of addresses of second-generation Moroccan men in Amsterdam and Rotterdam to cope with the rapid depletion of the address pool due to higher than expected non-response in that group. The sampling strategy is described below in four main stages.

In the first stage, one important substantive decision was to ensure that the sample design sampled members of the two ethnic groups – second-generation Turks and Moroccans – and the comparison group in the same context, i.e. neighbourhood. The survey objective was to generate statistically representative results at the level of both cities. In probability samples, all elements (i.e. neighbourhoods and ethnic group members) must have a non-zero chance of selection, so that neighbourhoods included in the sampling frame must have members of each of the three groups as residents. In general, the probability of selecting a member of a particular study group is determined by the product of the following two chances: (1) that a member of a particular study group is selected within the neighbourhood and (2) that the neighbourhood is selected from the sampling frame of neighbourhoods. The issue of sample selection is taken up in detail below.

Not all neighbourhoods of the two cities were included in the sampling frame. Consultation of population statistics published by the municipal population register (GBA) showed that two neighbourhoods in Amsterdam and eleven neighbourhoods in Rotterdam did not have members of all three groups as residents, and thus were excluded from the sampling frame. However, it must be noted that the excluded neighbourhoods are very sparsely populated, totalling only 104 inhabitants in Amsterdam and 523 in Rotterdam, as most of these neighbourhoods are industrial areas.[1] Thus, bearing the above in mind, the survey results are statistically representative of more than 99.5 per cent of all members of study groups living in both cities. Put more precisely, the survey results are representative of all members of the three study groups who live in the neighbourhoods included in the sampling frames of both cities.

A closer look at the spatial distribution of Turkish and Moroccan ethnic group residents in both cities shows that there is high correlation ($r^2 = .95$ and $r^2 = .87$ in Amsterdam and Rotterdam, respectively). Because of this, the combined total of Turkish and Moroccan ethnic group residents in the age range 15-44 (in Amsterdam) and age range 18-35 (in Rotterdam) was taken as a measure of size (MOS)[2] for the 90 and 77 neighbourhoods in Amsterdam and Rotterdam, respectively, and to represent the distribution of unobserved numbers of second-generation Turks and Moroccans in both cities.[3] In this way, neighbourhoods could be sampled with selection probabilities proportional to this measure of size, so that areas with higher concentrations of Turkish and Moroccan ethnic group members would be allocated a larger proportion of the gross sample size. Once neighbourhoods are sampled, fixed numbers of addresses (i.e. clusters; see below) of Turks, Moroccans and Dutch people would then be sampled within these neighbourhoods.

In a second stage, a decision was taken on cluster size: 30 personal addresses would comprise three groups, each with ten persons of Turkish descent, ten of Moroccan descent and ten of Dutch descent. This size was a compromise guided by two main interests. The first concern was to avoid the risk of drawing a 'bad' sample of neighbourhoods, which would be more likely if the cluster size was large. The threat of running this risk would have thus limited the number of neighbourhoods to be sampled. The second concern was indeed to ensure that a sufficient number of neighbourhoods would be sampled, allowing survey results to be aggregated to the next higher administrative/planning level, the *stadsdeel* ('city district'). This would allow the *stadsdelen* to be compared, for instance, in matters regarding the differential effect that city policies have on integration variables.

In a third stage, the systematic selection method was applied to the geographically sorted list of neighbourhoods, separately for each city, to ensure an optimal spatial spread of the sample over cities and neighbourhoods. As the minimum effective sample size for each city was set at 750 respondents, 750/30 = 25 clusters would need to be allocated to neighbourhoods by means of the systematic selection method or, in other words, allocation. Using the aforementioned population statistics on numbers of residents of Turkish and Moroccan descent in neighbourhoods, the list was transformed into a cumulative list of numbers of persons of these two ethnic groups. A sampling interval (k) was then computed, and a random start number obtained, so that all 25 clusters could be allocated to the neighbourhoods in a random manner (i.e. every k-th neighbourhood, e.g. see Cochran 1977: 205-231). This resulted in a sample of 23 of the remaining 90 neighbourhoods in Amsterdam (about one in four) and 24 of the 77 neighbourhoods in Rotterdam (about 1 in 3). The method ensures that areas with large numbers of Turkish and Moroccan ethnic group members have a higher probability of being selected and could be selected even more than once. The latter is precisely what happened, and resulted in the allocation of two clusters (2 x 30 persons) to the same neighbourhood in two neighbourhoods in Amsterdam (Landlust and Geuzenveld) and in the case of one neighbourhood in Rotterdam (Nieuwe Westen). To compensate *a priori* for a potential non-response rate of 75 per cent, the actual cluster size was increased by a factor of four and therefore became 4x30 = 120 persons. Once neighbourhoods were sampled, the municipal population registers were requested to provide the actual numbers of second-generation Turks, Moroccans and the comparison group in the age range 18-35 years old residing in the sampled neighbourhoods, as well as in the city around the time of the selection of the sample (1 April 2006).

In the final stage, 1,000 addresses of members of each group living in the sampled neighbourhoods, totalling 6,000 addresses in both cities, were sampled from the population register. Because more than one second-generation person may live at the same address, it was decided to select only one person per ethnic group per address, using the last-birthday method (Kish 1965). This led to a reduction of the number of addresses of potential respondents. During fieldwork this number was reduced further to 4,999 addresses, mainly as a result of the fact that many addresses were no longer valid.[4] This number (n), the *gross effective sample size*, distributed over the sample neighbourhoods and ethnic groups, is presented in the table below. Eventually, completed or partially completed interviews were obtained from 1,505 persons (= *net effective sample size*), implying an overall response rate of 30.1 per cent.

Table A.1 summarises main population and sample statistics such as the size of the second-generation Turks and Moroccans in both cities and of the comparison group at the time of sample selection in April 2006 and according to the municipal population register (GBA). Regarding representation, it can be deduced from the figures that the sampled neighbourhoods are home to more than 60 per cent of the second-generation Turks and Moroccans residing in these cities (e.g. Amsterdam, second-generation Turks (3,266/5,088) × 100 = 64.2 per cent). In a similar way, it can be deduced from these figures that about one in three members of the comparison group lives in the sampled neighbourhoods.

The way the sample was allocated according to cities, ethnic groups and neighbourhoods, and the finding that response rates differed considerably between neighbourhoods and cities, imply that the design and implementation was non-self-weighting. Therefore, an *ex post* correction factor or compensation *weight* was allocated to each of the 1,505 respondents. This weight consists of several components, each reflecting a stage in sample design and implementation leading to unequal selection probabilities, such as the allocation of the sample to cities, ethnic groups, neighbourhoods and clusters, and the finding that response rates varied considerably across cities, ethnic groups and neighbourhoods. The average weights of the second-generation Turks and Moroccan respondents appeared to be 0.348 and 0.354, respectively, and for the comparison group, 2.258. These compensation weights were eventually used to produce the results in this report, meaning that the presented figures are reflective of second-generation Turks and Moroccans and members of the comparison groups in the two cities (ESS 2007; Purdon & Pickering 2001; Lee et al. 1989).

Table A.1 Reference population, sample design and implementation statistics of study groups in Amsterdam and Rotterdam

	Amsterdam				Rotterdam				Total
	Turks	Moroccans	Comparison group	Total	Turks	Moroccans	Comparison group	Total	
City population				743,024				588,718	1,331,742
Ethnic group population	38,337	65,426	382,746	486,509	45,415	36,831	317,943	400,189	886,698
Second generation, all ages	16,539	30,588			22,562	14,560			
Second generation, 18-35	5,088	8,649	102,491	116,228	6,941	4,117	71,288	82,346	198,574
Second generation 18-35 in sampled neighbourhoods	3,266	5,398	29,351	38,015	4,772	2,655	24,003	31,430	69,445
Sample									
Target number of respondents	250	250	250	750	250	250	250	750	1,500
Neighborhoods sampled				23 of 90				24 of 77	47 of 167
Gross effective number of addresses sampled	792	935	646	2,373	863	1,036	727	2,626	4,999
Succesfully interviewed respondents	237	242	259	738	263	251	253	767	1,505
Response %	29.9	25.9	40.1	31.1	30.5	24.2	34.8	29.2	30.1

1.2 TIES survey implementation

The fieldwork in the two cities lasted almost fourteen months, from May 2006 through July 2007. The fieldwork was organised, implemented and documented by Bureau Veldkamp in Amsterdam (Schothorst 2007), in close consultation and collaboration with NIDI staff. In a pilot phase, the questionnaire was tested and adjusted after interviewing twelve respondents belonging to the intended ethnic and age groups. In total, 83 interviewers (43 in Amsterdam and 40 in Rotterdam) were recruited and trained to conduct the interview with a portable computer (CAPI). Interviewers were mainly Dutch, and many of them had served as professional interviewers and had experience with interviewing members of ethnic minority groups. In addition to their training on the subject matter covered by the questionnaire and on the code of conduct, interviewers were instructed to pay particular attention to verifying whether the potential respondent at the address they received was indeed the person whom they were about to interview. This issue is of particular relevance because it is estimated that between 10 and 20 per cent of the housing accommodation, notably in Amsterdam, is rented out by the registered tenant or owner to a third party, without formal notification to the register. Shortly before the interviewers went into the field, invitation letters were sent to all sampled person addresses in which the objectives of the study and interview were explained, the importance of cooperation stressed, and the forthcoming visit of an interviewer announced. Mentioned, too, was the fact that respondents would receive ten euros as a token of gratitude for their collaboration.

Overall, obtaining a successful interview from the sampled respondents proved to be a cumbersome undertaking. The main problems encountered were:
- Addresses (at a rate of almost 15 per cent) appeared to no longer be valid (potential respondent had moved elsewhere or died).
- Difficulties in actually reaching the doorstep of potential respondents, particularly in large apartment buildings.
- Suspiciousness and sometimes even hostility on the part of potential respondents.
- Length and complexity of the questionnaire, as well as coverage of topics that were perceived by respondents to be 'sensitive'. A typical interview would take about one hour and fifteen minutes, leading to a low total output of between 24 and 50 interviews per week.
- Respondents trying to postpone the interview in hopes that the interviewer would eventually abort the appointment. The general rule was that the interviewer should try at least five times to fulfil an interview appointment with potential respondents.

Among others, the following measures were taken to improve fieldwork performance:
- Reducing interview time by dropping certain questions from the questionnaire.
- Splitting the interview into two components: a face-to-face CAPI interview and the written version of the CAPI questionnaire, which the respondent completed in private and on the spot or in private though at some later time and to be submitted to the survey bureau (this was considered mix-mode interviewing). Furthermore, an online webpage-based version of the questionnaire was developed, so that respondents had control over when they responded to the questionnaire. Overall, 50 per cent of the completed interviews came from CAPI face-to-face interviews, 42 per cent from mix-mode interviews and 8 per cent from online interviews.
- To deal with refusal/non-response conversion, various measures were taken to retrieve an interview from respondents: a reminder invitation-to-participate letter, an increase of the token gift to twenty euros, providing additional training to interviewers in 'persuasion communication techniques and strategies'.[5]

1.3 TIES survey evaluation

Although the overall response rates in the two cities are similar, averaging 30.1 per cent (see Table A.1), differences between the groups are considerable. In both cities, respondents of the Moroccan ethnic group performed the poorest with, on average, a 25.0 per cent response rate in the sampled neighbourhoods, as compared with the 30.2 per cent and 37.3 per cent response rates of members of the Turkish second generation and the comparison group. Analysis of response rates by neighbourhood showed that such rates vary considerably between neighbourhoods, and that it mattered whether a member of a particular ethnic group was contacted in one neighbourhood or in another. For instance, in Rotterdam, the response rate of the second-generation Moroccans in the Spangen neighbourhood was twice as high (50.0 per cent) as the response rate of that same study group in the nearby neighbourhood of Oude Noorden (23.1 per cent). This large discrepancy may be due to general differences in the personal characteristics of ethnic group members living in different neighbourhoods, due to particular neighbourhood characteristics or due to inconsistencies in interviewer performance.

As non-response was high in the survey, it is worth looking at differences between respondents and non-respondents. Often this is a difficult undertaking because not much is known about the characteristics

APPENDIX: SAMPLE DESIGN, TIES SURVEY

Table A.2 Differences between respondents (R.) and non-respondents (N.R.) regarding characteristics recorded in municipal population registers (GBA)

		Turks			Moroccans			Comparison group			Total population
		R.	N.R.	Total	R.	N.R.	Total	R.	N.R.	Total	
Sex	Male	48.4	54.4	52.6	41.4	49.4	47.4	49.2	51.6	50.7	50.2
	Female	51.6	45.6	47.4	58.6	50.6	52.6	50.8	48.4	49.3	49.8
	Total	100.0	100.0	100.0	100.0	100.0	100.0	100.0	100.0	100.0	100.0
Age	18-19	17.8	17.9	17.9	26.9	21.8	23.0	7.8	7.2	7.4	16.7
	20-24	39.0	42.0	41.1	43.3	46.5	45.7	25.6	24.9	25.1	38.0
	25-29	32.0	29.7	30.4	21.7	24.1	23.5	30.1	33.3	32.1	28.5
	30-34	11.2	10.4	10.6	8.1	7.6	7.8	36.5	34.6	35.4	16.8
	Total	100.0	100.0	100.0	100.0	100.0	100.0	100.0	100.0	100.0	100.0
	Mean	24.4	24.2	24.3	23.3	23.5	23.5	27.5	27.5	27.5	24.9
	Standard error	0.2	0.1	0.1	0.2	0.1	0.1	0.2	0.2	0.1	0.1
Marital status	Never married	56.6	68.5	64.9	77.6	78.2	78.1	86.3	88.5	87.7	76.2
	Married	40.6	27.8	31.7	20.5	19.0	19.3	11.9	9.5	10.4	21.1
	Separated	2.8	3.6	3.4	1.9	2.7	2.5	1.8	2.0	1.9	2.6
	Divorced		0.1	0.1		0.2	0.1				0.1
	Total	100.0	100.0	100.0	100.0	100.0	100.0	100.0	100.0	100.0	100.0
	Total N	500	1,155	1,655	420	1,240	1,660	512	861	1,373	4,688

Note: Records of Moroccan men who were included in the supplementary sample of June 2007 are excluded from this table.

of non-respondents. However, population registers hold some information that can be used to make a basic comparison between respondents and non-respondents. This is shown in Table A.2.

As compared to the situation in the general population of both cities (last column), men are overrepresented among non-respondents in all groups, most notably, among the second-generation Moroccans. As a consequence, women are somewhat overrepresented in the dataset of 1,505 successfully interviewed persons. Age does not seem to be a discriminating factor in all three groups when it comes to comparing respondents and non-respondents. It is interesting to note, though, that members of the comparison group are, on average, three to four years older than members of the other two groups, which may be relevant to the interpretation and explanation of differences found between ethnic groups regarding certain socioeconomic survey characteristics. Furthermore, married or cohabiting persons are somewhat overrepresented among responding persons, notably among the second-generation Turks, which is not surprising, as such people tend to be at home more often and thus more likely to come into contact with a visiting interviewer. Thus, differences between respondents and non-respondents regarding personal characteristics as recorded in the population register are slight and match expectations.

Notes

1   In brackets the total populations (as of 1 January 2006) of Amsterdam's excluded neighbourhoods are given: Spieringhorn (2), Bedrijventerrein Sloterdijk (102); Rotterdam: Noord Kethel (74), Kralingse Bos (128), Rijnpoort (79), Spaanse polder (176), Eemhaven (29), Waalhaven-Zuid (12), Botlek (3), Europoort (5), Maasvlakte (0), Bedrijvenemp. RNW (17), Rivium (0).
2   Differences in age range of MOS data are due to inconsistencies between the two municipalities' inclusion of details in their published data.
3   The latter are smaller in number because the age range 18-35 also includes first-generation individuals (e.g. brides and grooms of second-generation Turks and Moroccans who are brought over from Turkey or Morocco).
4   Due to problems and delays in fieldwork operations, the survey period extended to about thirteen months (May 2006-June 2007). With the relatively high mobility of persons in the age range 18-35, it came as no surprise that interviewers were often unable to locate an intended respondent at his or her given address, particularly if there was a long time lapse between selection of the sample (1 April 2006) and the intended interview date. In this regard, population register staff point out that the validity of provided sample addresses becomes questionable if used beyond a period of more than two months.
5   There are limits to refusal/non-response conversion in that such efforts tend to focus on persons who are the 'easiest' to 'convert', contributing to selection bias (Stoop 2005).

References

BPR (2006), The Municipal Personal Records Database. www.bprbzk.nl/ content.jsp?objectid = 4011. Ministerie van Binnenlandse Zaken en Koninkrijksrelaties.

Cochran, W. (1977), *Sampling Techniques*, third edition. New York: Wiley and Sons.

Crok, S, J. Slot, T. Fedorova, M. Janssen & L. ten Broeke (2004), *Naar burgerschap in Amsterdam. Diversiteits- en integratiemonitor 2004*. Gemeente Amsterdam, Dienst Onderzoek en Statistiek.

ESS (2004), ESS2-2004 Deviations and Fieldwork Summary. http://ess.nsd.uib.no/index.jsp?year = 2005&module = fworksummary.

ESS (2007), Weighting European Social Survey Data. http://ess.nsd.uib.no/files/WeightingESS.pdf.

Gemeente Amsterdam (2006), *De Marokkaanse gemeenschap in Amsterdam*. Dienst Onderzoek en Statistiek.

Heer, W. de & E.D. de Leeuw (1999), 'Enquêteren bij personen en huishoudens, een bewogen geschiedenis' in B. Erwich & J.G.S.J. van Maarseveen (eds.), *Een eeuw statistieken. Historisch-methodologische schetsen van de Nederlandse officiële statistieken in de twintigste eeuw*. Voorburg: CBS.

Kish, L. (1965), *Survey Sampling*. New York: John Wiley & Sons, Inc.

Lee, E.S., R. Forthhofer & R. Lorimor (1989), *Analyzing Complex Survey Data*, Sage University Paper series on Quantitative Applications in the Social Sciences, series no. 07-071. Newbury Park CA: Sage.

Purdon, S. & K. Pickering (2001), *The use of sampling weights in the analysis of the 1998 Workplace Employee Relations Survey*. London: National Centre for Social Research.

Schmeets, H. & R. van der Bie (eds.) (2005), *Enquêteonderzoek onder allochtonen. Problemen en oplossingen*. Voorburg/Heerlen: CBS.

Schothorst, Y. (2007), *Veldwerkverslag, TIES project*. Amsterdam: Veldkamp Survey Bureau.

Stoop, I.A.L. (2005), *The hunt for the last respondent. Non-response in sample surveys*. SCP-report 2005/8. The Hague.

Conclusies en aanbevelingen[1]

Maurice Crul, George Groenewold en Liesbeth Heering

De Nederlandse tweede generatie van Turkse en Marokkaanse afkomst is momenteel volwassen aan het worden en de oudere cohorten hebben inmiddels de overstap van het onderwijs naar de arbeidsmarkt gemaakt. Dit betekent dat we nu voor het eerst werkelijk de balans op kunnen maken van de positie die de tweede generatie inneemt in de Nederlandse samenleving. Het TIES project behandelt dit vraagstuk door een grote verscheidenheid aan onderwerpen te onderzoeken. De primaire interesse richt zich op de aspecten van *structurele* integratie, zoals de toegang tot en deelname aan het onderwijs en de arbeidsmarkt. Daarnaast richt het onderzoek zich op onderwerpen die van belang zijn voor de *sociale* integratie, zoals sociale relaties, partnerkeuze en gezinsvorming, religie en identiteit. Het TIES onderzoek is uitgevoerd in de twee grootste steden, Amsterdam en Rotterdam, onder drie verschillende groepen respondenten: de in Nederland geboren kinderen van immigranten uit Turkije en Marokko en een vergelijkingsgroep van jongeren met twee in Nederland geboren ouders. De leeftijd van de respondenten ligt tussen de achttien en 35 jaar.

In dit rapport wordt steeds de term vergelijkingsgroep gebruikt, en niet de term 'Nederlanders'. De belangrijkste reden hiervoor is het feit dat de respondenten van de tweede generatie betrokken bij het TIES onderzoek – per definitie – geboren zijn in Nederland en in veel gevallen ook de Nederlandse nationaliteit hebben.

Op het gebied van onderwijs en de arbeidsmarkt weerspiegelt het dominante beeld van de tweede generatie in de publieke opinie afwisselend bezorgdheid en optimisme. Het is het klassieke dilemma: is het glas halfvol of halfleeg? De belangrijkste uitkomsten van ons onderzoek laten zien dat dit dilemma ook de realiteit weerspiegelt: een aanzienlijk deel van de tweede generatie doet het zeer goed, terwijl een ander deel duidelijk achter blijft. Misschien wel de meest opvallende uitkomst is de sterke mate van polarisatie *binnen* de tweede generatie groepen.

Het is een gegeven dat een korte onderwijsloopbaan een belangrijke indicator voor achterstand is. Onder de jongeren die hun onderwijscarrière reeds hebben afgesloten is de groep die geen startkwalificatie behaalde aanzienlijk: ongeveer de helft. Een startkwalificatie wordt gedefinieerd als het minimum onderwijsniveau dat succesvol moet zijn afgesloten om een kans te maken op de arbeidsmarkt. De jongeren zonder een dergelijke startkwalificatie worden officieel gezien als 'risicojongeren'. Zij vormen ongeveer een kwart van onze onderzoekspopulatie. Zoals te verwachten valt zijn zij ook prominent aanwezig in de groep die langdurig werkloos is en blijven vaak afhankelijk van een uitkering. Getrouwde vrouwen, wier belangrijkste activiteit het verzorgen van de kinderen is, zijn eveneens oververtegenwoordigd in deze groep. Deze situatie komt het meest voor onder de tweede generatie Turkse vrouwen.

Zij die succesvol zijn, volgen meestal nog onderwijs. Dit is het duidelijkst zichtbaar onder de tweede generatie Marokkanen die doorgegaan zijn met studeren en die nu te vinden zijn op het hbo en de universiteit, of die net de overgang van hoger onderwijs naar de arbeidsmarkt hebben gemaakt. De helft van de jongeren uit deze groep is niet direct doorgestroomd naar het hoger onderwijs, maar heeft een lange route afgelegd en heeft eerst vmbo of mavo gedaan, is daarna doorgegaan in het mbo om uiteindelijk in het hbo of aan de universiteit te studeren. Hun volharding en ambitie zijn karakteristiek. Zeker de vrouwen die het hoger onderwijs succesvol doorlopen hebben, vertalen hun onderwijsprestaties in goede posities op de arbeidsmarkt. Deze vrouwen stellen het huwelijk en het krijgen van kinderen uit. De gemiddelde huwelijksleeftijd onder Turkse en Marokkaanse vrouwen van de tweede generatie stijgt voornamelijk door dit fenomeen.

Een vergelijkbaar verschil tussen de tweede generatie Marokkanen en Turken wordt zichtbaar als we kijken naar de arbeidsmarktposities. Terwijl van de Turkse tweede generatie de grote meerderheid hun overstap naar de arbeidsmarkt al heeft gemaakt, is dit slechts voor de helft van de tweede generatie Marokkanen het geval. Bovendien zien we zowel positieve als negatieve uitkomsten op het gebied van de arbeidsmarkt. Werkloosheidscijfers zijn relatief hoog in beide tweede generatie groepen. Tien procent van de tweede generatie Turken is werkloos en actief op zoek zijn naar een baan, voor de tweede generatie Marokkanen ligt dit percentage op acht. Dit percentage ligt vier tot vijf keer hoger dan dat van de vergelijkingsgroep. Ook is de onderwijspositie van de vergelijkingsgroep veel beter: slechts tien procent heeft geen 'startkwalificatie' en kan beschouwd worden als voortijdig schoolverlater.

Tweede generatie Turken en Marokkanen die de overstap naar de arbeidsmarkt al gemaakt hebben werken voornamelijk in lager geschoolde en ongeschoolde beroepen. Maar één op de vijf heeft een hooggeschoolde of academisch geschoolde baan. Dit staat in sterk contrast met de vergelijkingsgroep waar meer dan de helft in deze twee categorieën terug te vinden is.

De Marokkaanse tweede generatie lijkt de slechtste positie in te nemen op de arbeidsmarkt omdat meer mensen een baan hebben in lagere ongeschoolde beroepen. Tegelijkertijd zijn in deze groep de jongste cohorten oververtegenwoordigd in ons onderzoek en – zoals hierboven al gesteld – studeren zij langer door dan tweede generatie Turken. Daarom kan de vergelijking wel eens drastisch veranderen op het moment dat de groep die nu nog in het hoger onderwijs studeert de overstap naar de arbeidsmarkt maakt.

Binnen de tweede generatie groepen doen de vrouwen het iets beter op de arbeidsmarkt dan de mannen. Zij werken vaker in de dienstverlenende beroepen zoals de gezondheidszorg, het sociaal werk en het onderwijs, sectoren waar momenteel een nijpend tekort aan arbeidskrachten is. Bovendien zijn, zeker in de grote steden, werkgevers in het bijzonder op zoek naar werknemers van verschillende culturele achtergrond om in te kunnen gaan op steeds grotere behoefte van de eerste generatie migranten op het gebied van sociale zorg en gezondheidszorg.

Als we kijken naar het inkomensniveau dan zien we dat de Turkse tweede generatie duidelijk voorop loopt vergeleken met de Marokkaanse tweede generatie. Dit kan opnieuw ten delen verklaard worden uit het feit dat een groter aantal tweede generatie Marokkanen nog in het onderwijs zit en dientengevolge leeft van een studiebeurs en wat kleine bijbaantjes. Wederom kunnen we voorspellen dat als de hoger opgeleide Marokkanen de arbeidsmarkt eenmaal betreden, het verschil tussen de Turkse en Marokkaanse tweede generatie waarschijnlijk verdwijnt, of zelfs kantelt. Een uiteindelijke conclusie kan dus pas getrokken worden na vervolgonderzoek.

De betere inkomenssituatie wordt ook zichtbaar in het grotere aandeel tweede generatie Turken dat in het bezit is van een eigen huis. Dit geldt voor een derde van de Turkse respondenten die geen deel meer uitmaken van het huishouden van hun ouders. In aanmerking genomen dat in grote steden als Amsterdam en Rotterdam het aandeel sociale huurwoningen zeer groot is, is dit een opmerkelijke bevinding. Tweede generatie Turkse huiseigenaren wonen vaker in eengezinswoningen dan de vergelijkingsgroep en bijna de helft woont in relatief nieuwe woningen (minder dan 25 jaar oud).

In lijn met de trend om vroeger het onderwijs te verlaten trouwen tweede generatie Turken ook op jongere leeftijd en krijgen zij ook jonger kinderen dan de tweede generatie Marokkanen. Meer dan de helft van de Turkse meisjes van de tweede generatie die het ouderlijk huis heeft verlaten, deed dat om te gaan trouwen. Daartegenover staat dat de grootste groep Marokkaanse meisjes van de tweede generatie die niet meer bij hun ouders wonen, het huis verliet om in het hoger onderwijs te gaan studeren of om zelfstandig te gaan wonen.

Met betrekking tot partnerkeuze en gezinsvorming lijkt de Turkse tweede generatie het sterkst georiënteerd op de eigen groep en het land van herkomst van de ouders. De jongeren vinden vaak hun partner via familievakanties of op feesten in de Turkse gemeenschap. Bij ongeveer de helft van de huwelijken hebben de Turkse ouders enige mate van positieve of negatieve druk uitgeoefend. Eén op de vijf partners is een bloedverwant. Ook op het gebied van de rolpatronen van man en vrouw lijkt de Turkse tweede generatie het meest traditioneel. Eenenveertig procent van de echtgenotes van de Turkse tweede generatie mannen is niet actief op de arbeidsmarkt, maar zorgt voor de kinderen. Onder de vergelijkingsgroep is het aandeel vrouwelijke partners dat werkt twee keer zo hoog. Interessant genoeg hebben ook de Marokkaanse mannen van de tweede generatie in meerderheid een partner die werkt. De meeste tweede generatie respondenten huwden iemand met hun eigen etnische achtergrond. De meest opvallende trend in dit geval is dat onze respondenten steeds vaker trouwen met iemand die, net als zij, uit de tweede generatie afkomstig is, hoewel nog steeds de meerderheid van de huwelijkspartners zelf migrant is.

Met betrekking tot identiteiten en identificatie bevestigt ons onderzoek de verwachting dat mensen zich tegelijkertijd op verschillende niveaus sterk kunnen identificeren. Zo blijkt voor de meeste respondenten een sterke groepsidentiteit (Marokkaans of Turks) zeer wel samen te gaan met een sterke lokale (Amsterdamse of Rotterdamse) of nationale (Nederlandse) identiteit. Hetzelfde geldt voor een sterke moslimidentiteit gecombineerd met een sterke lokale en nationale identiteit. De tweede generatie ziet deze duidelijk niet als elkaar uitsluitende identiteiten, al lijkt de huidige maatschappelijke discussie over dit onderwerp anders te suggereren. Wellicht als gevolg van het feit dat de locale identiteit minder betwist is, wordt deze bijzonder sterk gevoeld, zeker vergeleken met de nationale identiteit. Tweederde van de respondenten van de tweede generatie geeft aan een sterke of zeer sterke Amsterdamse of Rotterdamse identiteit te hebben. Voorts geven respondenten die nog bij hun ouders thuis wonen aan ook een sterke band met de buurt te hebben.

Religie is van groot belang in het leven van de tweede generatie Turken en Marokkanen. Dit geldt vooral voor de laatste groep, waarin bijna de helft van de respondenten stelt dat religie een grote rol speelt in hun leven. Dit betekent niet noodzakelijkerwijs dat de religieuze *praktijk* een even grote rol speelt: feitelijk ziet de meerderheid religie vooral als een persoonlijke zaak en bezoekt zelden of nooit de moskee. Een groot deel van de tweede generatie bidt nooit. Zij die wel elke dag of elke week bidden en actief zijn op andere religieuze gebieden vormen echter een niet onaanzienlijke minderheid van ongeveer een kwart van de respondenten van Turkse en Marokkaanse afkomst.

Een andere vraag is of hun religieuze identiteit zich vertaalt naar politieke gezichtspunten of in hun visie op de rol van man en vrouw. De tweede generatie verschilt weliswaar van de vergelijkingsgroep in hun visie op een aantal maatschappelijke kwesties, maar de gevonden verschillen zijn niet groot. Met betrekking tot onderwijs, bijvoorbeeld, denkt vrijwel geen respondent van de tweede generatie dat een opleiding voor mannen belangrijker is dan voor vrouwen. Slechts een kleine minderheid vindt dat vrouwen niet zouden moeten werken als zij kleine kinderen hebben (een opvatting die overigens ook niet ongewoon is onder autochtone conservatieven). Nog geen tien procent spreekt uit dat zij het problematisch zouden vinden om een vrouw als superieur te hebben op het werk. Slechts een kleine minderheid vindt dat de Islam een meer politieke rol in de samenleving zou moeten spelen.

Vaak wordt de groep die helemaal niet religieus is genegeerd. In de tweede generatie stelt echter één op de tien jongeren dat zij geen enkele religie hebben. Over het geheel genomen vormt de rol die religie speelt in hun levens het belangrijkste verschil tussen de tweede generatie groepen en de vergelijkingsgroep. Van de laatste groep zeggen acht op de tien jongeren dat zij geen enkele religie hebben. Dit contrast lijkt een grote uitdaging voor de grote steden te vormen. Het is in dit licht interessant dat de meerderheid van de vergelijkingsgroep instemt met de stelling dat het positief is als mensen van verschillende religies samenleven in de stad. Dit is echter één van de onderwerpen waarop de vergelijkingsgroepen uit Amsterdam en Rotterdam een aanmerkelijk verschillende mening zijn toegedaan. In Amsterdam onderschrijft 63 procent de stelling, in Rotterdam slechts 39 procent. Ook in andere stellingen over de multiculturele samenleving, uit de Rotterdamse vergelijkingsgroep zich veel negatiever en is minder geneigd om te onderkennen dat er sprake is van discriminatie op de arbeidsmarkt ten opzichte van mensen met een Turkse of Marokkaanse achtergrond. Het onderzoek lijkt dus het stereotype beeld van Amsterdam als meer tolerante stad te ondersteunen. Dit betekent echter niet dat de tweede generatie zich erg prettig voelt in Amsterdam. In het bijzonder de tweede generatie Marokkanen vinden dat er de laatste jaren een minder vriendelijk klimaat is ontstaan.

Implicaties van de onderzoeksresultaten

Voor beleidsmakers zal het meest verontrustende onderzoeksresultaat zijn dat een kwart van de tweede generatie niet in het bezit is van een 'startkwalificatie' voor de arbeidsmarkt. Hun maatschappelijke positie is zeer kwetsbaar en onzeker. In de 'zandloper' economie van de grote steden lopen zij groot risico op de bodem te blijven en zij zullen amper boven de economische positie van hun ouders uitkomen. Ze zullen hoogstwaarschijnlijk wonen in hetzelfde type woonwijken waarin zij zelf zijn opgegroeid, alleen zullen deze wijken nu nog meer gesegregeerd zijn. Hun kinderen zullen naar scholen gaan die vaak in de termen van de onderwijsinspectie de 'slecht presterende scholen' heten. Het is in dit verband ook problematisch dat de meerderheid een partner uit het land van herkomst van de ouders trouwt, die over het algemeen niet goed is toegerust voor de Nederlandse arbeidsmarkt. Zodoende ziet de toekomst voor dit kwart van de tweede generatie jongeren er niet veelbelovend uit. Vanwege hun onzekere positie op de arbeidsmarkt zullen zij zeer waarschijnlijk afhankelijk zijn van sociale huurwoningen, of zelfs van een uitkering en hun kinderen zullen opgroeien in een financiële situatie op de armoedegrens.

De relatief grote groep 'risicojongeren' onder de tweede generatie staat in sterk contrast met de vergelijkingsgroep die in meerderheid hoog is opgeleid en waar beide partners vaak werken. Dit leidt vanzelfsprekend ook tot aanzienlijke inkomensverschillen en dit zou de maatschappij kunnen splijten in een groep armen die voornamelijk uit mensen met een immigratie achtergrond bestaat en een voornamelijk 'witte' midden- en hogere klasse.

Het sleutelwoord in het voorkomen van deze situatie is onderwijs. Teveel kinderen van migranten verlaten school voortijdig. Het lukt de scholen niet om de jongeren binnen boord te houden. Zoals het TIES onderzoek laat zien volgde meer dan de helft van de 'risicojongeren' aanvankelijk het vmbo-t of hoger. Zij zouden daarom, gezien hun bewezen capaciteiten in het middelbaar onderwijs, in staat moeten zijn om een mbo-2 niveau of hoger te behalen. Het feit dat dit een grote groep niet lukt vormt een duidelijke aanwijzing dat er aanzienlijke institutionele problemen bestaan in het middelbaar beroepsonderwijs binnen het Nederlandse schoolsysteem.

Het opkomen van een middenklasse van mensen met een migratieachtergrond (om het even of deze nu van de eerste, tweede of derde generatie zijn), zal cruciaal voor de steden blijken te zijn in het keren van een mogelijke etnische polarisatie. De resultaten van het TIES onderzoek op dit vlak stemmen optimistisch. Iets minder dan een derde van de tweede generatie studeert in het hoger onderwijs of heeft al een studie in het hoger onderwijs succesvol afgesloten. Zij zullen in hun gemeenschappen de voortrekkers zijn op het gebied van de opwaartse sociale mobiliteit. Ze zijn te vinden in de betere banen, hebben een eigen bedrijf of zijn actief als vertegenwoordiger in migranten organisaties of religieuze organisaties. Ze trouwen op een latere leeftijd en hun partners zijn vaak eveneens hoog opgeleid en hebben een baan, dus zij hebben vaak een dubbel inkomen Ze verlaten vaak hun oude buurt, of gaan wonen in de betere delen van hun oude wijk. De kinderen van deze ouders zullen opgroeien in financieel stabiele middenklasse gezinnen en zij hebben daardoor goede vooruitzichten voor de toekomst. Bovendien ontwikkelen zij via hun studie en werk over het algemeen meer contacten buiten de eigen etnische gemeenschap.

Het is belangrijk om op te merken dat in de succesvolle tweede generatie groep velen de zogenaamde 'lange route' door het onderwijs hebben gevolgd. Zij begonnen in het lager beroepsonderwijs, gingen door met middelbaar beroepsonderwijs om uiteindelijk aan te komen in het hoger beroepsonderwijs en de universiteit. Het stapelen van opleidingen neemt drie jaar langer dan de directe route. De lange route was van oudsher eveneens belangrijk voor Nederlandse kinderen van de arbeidersklasse. Het is van belang dat deze route in Nederland bestaat, al vallen er veel kinderen in deze fase uit. Het feit dat veel succesvolle studenten uit het hoger onderwijs aanvankelijk een vmbo-advies kregen roept echter vragen op over de mechanismes in de toepassing van dat basisschool advies en de geldigheid ervan.

De overgang naar de arbeidsmarkt van de 'risico'-groep in ons onderzoek brengt onze aandacht op twee belangrijke inzichten. Enerzijds betaalt de arbeidsmarkt niet altijd uit wat er op het gebied van onderwijs is geïnvesteerd. Een deel van de laaggeschoolde respondenten heeft een vaste baan bemachtigd, of zelfs een baan op geschoold niveau. Hoe ze dit hebben bereikt zou onderwerp van verder onderzoek moeten zijn, maar het duidt op het *inclusieve* effect van de arbeidsmarkt. Aan de ander kant zijn er duidelijk ook *uitsluitende* effecten van de arbeidsmarkt, zoals discriminatie, waar de 'risico' groep het meest kwetsbaar voor is.

Met betrekking tot de polarisatie *binnen* de tweede generatie groepen tussen een groeiende succesvolle middenklasse en een stabiliserende 'risico' groep zullen de twee cruciale vragen voor de toekomst zijn of de steden de middenklasse tweede generatie groepen aan zich kunnen binden en indien dit mogelijk is, of deze groepen als een bindmiddel willen fungeren tussen de 'risico' groep en de bredere samenleving. Het gebruikmaken van hun sociale en culturele kapitaal zou wel eens beslissend kunnen zijn voor het bouwen van een sociaal samenhangende stedelijke samenleving.

En hoe staat het met de bereidwilligheid van de tweede generatie jongeren om deel uit te maken van de Nederlandse samenleving? Onze uitkomsten tonen aan dat bijna de helft van de tweede generatie het eens of zelfs volkomen eens is met de stelling dat migranten en hun kinderen buitenshuis *zoveel mogelijk* volgens de Nederlandse normen en waarden zouden moeten leven. Het is een omvangrijke groep die een dergelijke sterke uitspraak ondersteunt. Tegelijkertijd vindt echter een grote groep van hen dat migranten en hun kinderen ook zoveel mogelijk naar de Turkse of Marokkaanse normen en waarden moet leven buitenshuis. Wellicht maken zij een onderscheid tussen hun gedrag in de publieke ruimte ten opzichte van hun eigen groep (bijvoorbeeld op een bruiloftsfeest) en ten opzichte van mensen van Nederlandse afkomst.

Tegelijkertijd is één op de vijf tweede generatie jongeren het *niet eens* met de stelling dat migranten en hun kinderen buitenshuis zoveel mogelijk volgens de Nederlandse normen en waarden zouden moeten leven. In plaats daarvan stellen zij dat Turkse en Marokkaanse migranten en hun kinderen volgens de Turkse of Marokkaanse normen en waarden moet leven buitenshuis. Deze positie beperkt hun interactie met andere etnische groepen vanzelfsprekend aanzienlijk. Van een even groot belang is echter de houding van de meerderheidssamenleving. Hier wijzen de verschillen tussen de vergelijkingsgroep in Rotterdam en Amsterdam, in hun houding ten opzichte van de multiculturele samenleving en migranten in het algemeen, op een verschil in stadscontext.

Het is van belang om te benadrukken dat we niet alleen moeten kijken naar de relatie tussen de tweede generatie groepen en de groep die vaak wordt aangeduid als 'van Nederlandse afkomst'. In de grote steden is in toenemende mate sprake van diversiteit en zeker in de jongere leeftijdscategorieën vormt de groep met een 'Nederlandse afkomst' een minderheid zoals alle anderen. Dus een deel van het klimaat waarin de tweede generatie Turken en Marokkanen opgroeien in Rotterdam en Amsterdam wordt ook gevormd door hun relaties met de grote gemeenschappen uit ondermeer Nederlands-Indië, Suriname, de Antillen en andere landen. Daarnaast vormen mensen met een gemengde etnische afkomst ook een steeds groter deel van de stedelijke realiteit. Een kwart van de vergelijkingsgroep in ons onderzoek heeft al een partner met een 'niet-Nederlandse' afkomst.

Tot slot laat het TIES survey zien dat het de mensen van de vergelijkingsgroep zijn die feitelijk de nieuwkomers zijn in de stad. In tegenstelling tot de tweede generatie groepen zijn zij in merendeel *niet* geboren en/of opgegroeid in Amsterdam of Rotterdam. Zij zijn het dus vooral die zich moeten aanpassen aan de nieuwe stad en zij zouden met meer recht nieuwkomers genoemd kunnen worden in de twee steden, ook gezien het gegeven dat velen van hen de stad op een gegeven moment weer zullen verlaten vanwege hun werk of wanneer ze een gezin vormen.

Noot

1   Dit hoofdstuk is de Nederlandse vertaling van hoofdstuk 9 van dit boek.

List of contributors

Maurice Crul, International Coordinator of the TIES project and Senior Researcher, Institute for Migration and Ethnic Studies, Amsterdam
   m.r.j.crul@uva.nl

Liesbeth Heering, International Coordinator of the TIES survey and Senior Researcher, Netherlands Interdisciplinary Demographic Institute, The Hague
   heering@nidi.nl

George Groenewold, Senior Researcher, Netherlands Interdisciplinary Demographic Institute, The Hague
   groenewold@nidi.nl

Helga de Valk, Senior Researcher, Institute for Migration and Ethnic Studies, Amsterdam, Netherlands Interdisciplinary Demographic Institute, The Hague
   valk@nidi.nl

Jeannette Schoorl, Senior Researcher, Netherlands Interdisciplinary Demographic Institute, The Hague
   schoorl@nidi.nl

Carlo van Praag, Fellow, Netherlands Interdisciplinary Demographic Institute, The Hague
   praag@nidi.nl

Gijs Beets, Senior Researcher, Netherlands Interdisciplinary Demographic Institute, The Hague
   beets@nidi.nl

Susan ter Bekke, Research Assistant, Netherlands Interdisciplinary Demographic Institute, The Hague
   bekke@nidi.nl

Other IMISCOE titles

IMISCOE Research

Rinus Penninx, Maria Berger, Karen Kraal, Eds.
*The Dynamics of International Migration and Settlement in Europe:
A State of the Art*
2006 (ISBN 978 90 5356 866 8)
(originally appearing in IMISCOE Joint Studies)

Leo Lucassen, David Feldman, Jochen Oltmer, Eds.
Paths of Integration: Migrants in Western Europe (1880-2004)
2006 (ISBN 978 90 5356 883 5)

Rainer Bauböck, Eva Ersbøll, Kees Groenendijk, Harald Waldrauch, Eds.
*Acquisition and Loss of Nationality: Policies and Trends in 15 European
Countries, Volume 1: Comparative Analyses*
2006 (ISBN 978 90 5356 920 7)

Rainer Bauböck, Eva Ersbøll, Kees Groenendijk, Harald Waldrauch, Eds.
*Acquisition and Loss of Nationality: Policies and Trends in 15 European
Countries, Volume 2: Country Analyses*
2006 (ISBN 978 90 5356 921 4)

Rainer Bauböck, Bernhard Perchinig, Wiebke Sievers, Eds.
Citizenship Policies in the New Europe
2007 (ISBN 978 90 5356 922 1)

Veit Bader
Secularism or Democracy? Associational Governance of Religious Diversity
2007 (ISBN 978 90 5356 999 3)

Holger Kolb & Henrik Egbert, Eds.
*Migrants and Markets: Perspectives from Economics and the Other
Social Sciences*
2008 (ISBN 978 90 5356 684 8)

Ralph Grillo, Ed.
*The Family in Question: Immigrant and Ethnic Minorities in
Multicultural Europe*
2008 (ISBN 978 90 5356 869 9)

Corrado Bonifazi, Marek Okólski, Jeannette Schoorl, Patrick Simon, Eds.
International Migration in Europe: New Trends and New Methods of Analysis
2008 (ISBN 978 90 5356 894 1)

IMISCOE Reports

Rainer Bauböck, Ed.
Migration and Citizenship: Legal Status, Rights and Political Participation
2006 (ISBN 978 90 5356 888 0)

Michael Jandl, Ed.
*Innovative Concepts for Alternative Migration Policies:
Ten Innovative Approaches to the Challenges of Migration in the 21st Century*
2007 (ISBN 978 90 5356 990 0)

Jeroen Doomernik & Michael Jandl, Eds.
Modes of Migration Regulation and Control in Europe
2008 (ISBN 978 90 5356 689 3)

IMISCOE Dissertations

Panos Arion Hatziprokopiou
Globalisation, Migration and Socio-Economic Change in Contemporary Greece: Processes of Social Incorporation of Balkan Immigrants in Thessaloniki
2006 (ISBN 978 90 5356 873 6)

Floris Vermeulen
The Immigrant Organising Process: Turkish Organisations in Amsterdam and Berlin and Surinamese Organisations in Amsterdam, 1960-2000
2006 (ISBN 978 90 5356 875 0)

Anastasia Christou
*Narratives of Place, Culture and Identity:
Second-Generation Greek-Americans Return 'Home'*
2006 (ISBN 978 90 5356 878 1)

Katja Rušinović
Dynamic Entrepreneurship: First and Second-Generation Immigrant Entrepreneurs in Dutch Cities
2006 (ISBN 978 90 5356 972 6)

Ilse van Liempt
Navigating Borders: Inside Perspectives on the Process of Human Smuggling into the Netherlands
2007 (ISBN 978 90 5356 930 6)

Myriam Cherti
Paradoxes of Social Capital: A Multi-Generational Study of Moroccans in London
2008 (ISBN 978 90 5356 032 7)

Marc Helbling
Practising Citizenship and Heterogeneous Nationhood: Naturalisations in Swiss Municipalities
2008 (ISBN 978 90 8964 034 5)